RANTS to REVELATIONS

Unabashedly Honest Reflections on Life, Spirituality and the Meaning of God

Ogun R. Holder

Illustrations by David Hayward

RANTS to REVELATIONS

Unabashedly Honest Reflections on Life, Spirituality and the Meaning of God

Ogun R. Holder

Illustrations by David Hayward

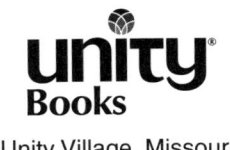

Unity Village, Missouri

Rants to Revelations
First Edition

Copyright © 2012 by Ogun R. Holder. All rights reserved. No part of this book may be used or reproduced in any manner without written permission from Unity Books, except in the case of brief quotations embedded in critical articles and reviews or in newsletters and lesson plans of licensed Unity teachers and ministers. For information, write to Unity Books, 1901 NW Blue Parkway, Unity Village, MO 64065-0001.

Unity Books are available at special discounts for bulk purchases for study groups, book clubs, sales promotions, book signings or fundraising. To place an order, call the Unity Customer Care Department at 1-866-236-3571 or email *wholesaleaccts@unityonline.org*.

Cover design: Design, Tom Truman; Photo, Terry Newell
Interior design: The Covington Group, Kansas City, Missouri

Library of Congress Control Number: 2012947660

ISBN: 978-0-87159-363-4

Canada BN 13252 0933 RT

*For Jennifer and Joy,
who love me
in spite of myself.*

ACKNOWLEDGMENTS

I am grateful for the family, friends, ministers and spiritual communities who have supported me in countless ways on my life's journey. Special thanks to Rev. Eileen Goor (my first Unity minister, mentor, cheerleader, friend), Rev. Dr. Thomas Shepherd (whose class assignment birthed this project), Alice Osborn (friend and editor, in that order), and my wife and daughter for exemplifying patience during this longer-than-I-promised process.

CONTENTS

Intro	....	xi
1 - DJ JC	....	1
2 - It's Me, Isn't It?	....	11
3 - God Wants Me to Do *What*?	....	23
4 - What Century Is This Anyway?	....	31
5 - Poor Parenting in Progress	....	39
6 - Jesus, Santa and the Flying Spaghetti Monster	....	49
7 - Loving and Letting Go	....	57
8 - I Survived Lent and All I Got Was This Lousy Enlightenment	....	65
9 - I Am *Awesome*!	....	73
10 - Find Your Passion, Find Your Peace	....	81
11 - You Got This!	....	91
12 - We Should Repeal the Law of Attraction	....	97
13 - Put Your Money Where Your Heart Is	....	105
14 - Better Me, Better Us	....	117
15 - Bah, Humbug!	....	129
16 - Zombies Need Love Too	....	139
17 - This Sucks!	....	147
18 - The Church Is Dead! Long Live the Church!	....	155
Outro	....	167
Endnotes	....	169
About the Author	....	175

INTRO

Hi.

My name is Ogun.

I'm a minister.

I like to write.

This is a book about me.

This is also a book about God.

I'm pretty sure I haven't figured out either one yet.

That was probably not what you expected a minister to say. Most ministers who write books are pretty sure about what they are saying about themselves and God. The only thing I'm sure about is that I'm not absolutely sure about anything. That's not to say I don't believe in anything—I believe in plenty. But to hold on to a belief for no reason other than I've always believed it isn't healthy on many levels. To throw out a belief at every passing fad is just as detrimental. I reside somewhere in the middle. I believe we should always examine our beliefs, refine them; hone them. Questions are good for that. I like to ask a lot of questions, especially about the things I think I'm sure about. My questions either lead me to a deeper conviction or shake my foundations to the point that I am forever changed. I live in the question.

I'm also a chronic oversharer (just follow my tweets *@ogunholder* if you think I'm exaggerating). Despite my fondness for volunteering unsolicited life updates, when people asked me what I was doing, I hesitated to tell them I was writing a book. Their response was usually in two parts. First, there was "Really!?" I was never sure if it was a question or an exclamation, or both. Depending on the look on their faces, it was either excitement about the prospect or incredulity that I could possibly have anything to write about. Invariably, the second part of the response was, "What's the book about?" Here things got a little dicey. At first I used to say "A memoir," but then I got the "you're-too-young-to-be-writing-a-memoir" look, which was a thought I'd had myself about a thousand times. Then I started saying, "I'm writing a spiritual memoir," to which their mouths would say, "Oh, that sounds interesting," but their faces would say, "What does that even mean? And aren't you too young to be writing a memoir?"

Sometimes I'd say I was working on a "humorous collection of spiritual anecdotes and insights." Again, the look. Plus that meant I had to be funny, which, besides assuming too much of myself, is no laughing matter (See what I mean about the assuming?). So then I started saying I was taking some of my blog posts and expanding on them, to which I'd often get, "Oh, you have a blog? What's that about?" And we'd start the routine all over again. Finally, a good friend asked me, "Do you even know what you're writing about?" My face said, "Pshaw! Don't be ridiculous! Of course I know what I'm writing about! How dare you ask?! What kind of friend are you?" Meanwhile, my mouth said nothing.

Wait ... aren't introductions supposed to inspire the reader to delve further into the book? Not sure I'm doing a good job so far, but it's my first book, so give me some leeway, please. The truth is I'm telling the only story I have the full authority and qualifications to tell: my own. It's not such a fantastic story. I don't see a made-for-TV or direct-to-DVD version anytime soon ... or ever (although if that were to happen, Taye Diggs is my first choice to play me; the resemblance is uncanny). I think my life is quite mundane compared to other people I know. But it's the only story I have, and it has its moments. In a word, it's a story of transformation. In more than a word, it's a story of how spirituality continues to transform my life into something I look forward to seeing more of tomorrow. Some of those moments of transformation came easily, some not so much, but all are valuable beyond measure.

Spirituality is one of those loaded words. It's maybe not as loaded as *religion*; it's definitely not as loaded as *God*. When I say *spirituality*, I'm talking about the presence and practice of God in my life. Yes, I believe we have to practice God since we're not all that great at it. When I say *God*, I mean ... well, that's a whole book unto itself, and it so happens I'm writing one! Like every other thought someone has had about God, everything you are going to read is unequivocally and indisputably correct. And it's also totally wrong. God is one of those things we can only figure out for ourselves, and the closer we think we get, the further we discover we have to go.

I have not been alive long enough to write tomes of life experiences (Volumes II and III, perhaps?), but I have come to a few realizations. For starters, my life is a perpetually unfolding expression of my spirit. My spirit is a perpetually unfolding expression of what I believe about God. What I believe about God ... well, that's the story of my life—a life that began on the tiny Caribbean island of Barbados but would outgrow it soon enough. I mentioned the "practice of God." I believe that's what life is: putting God into practice. It doesn't matter how much we believe in God; everyone believes something about God, and their life is informed by it. You're about to find out how much my incessantly evolving understanding of God has informed many aspects of my life. My hope is that it inspires you to contemplate the same for yours.

So let's get this party started ...

1

DJ JC

→ The Question of Prayer ←

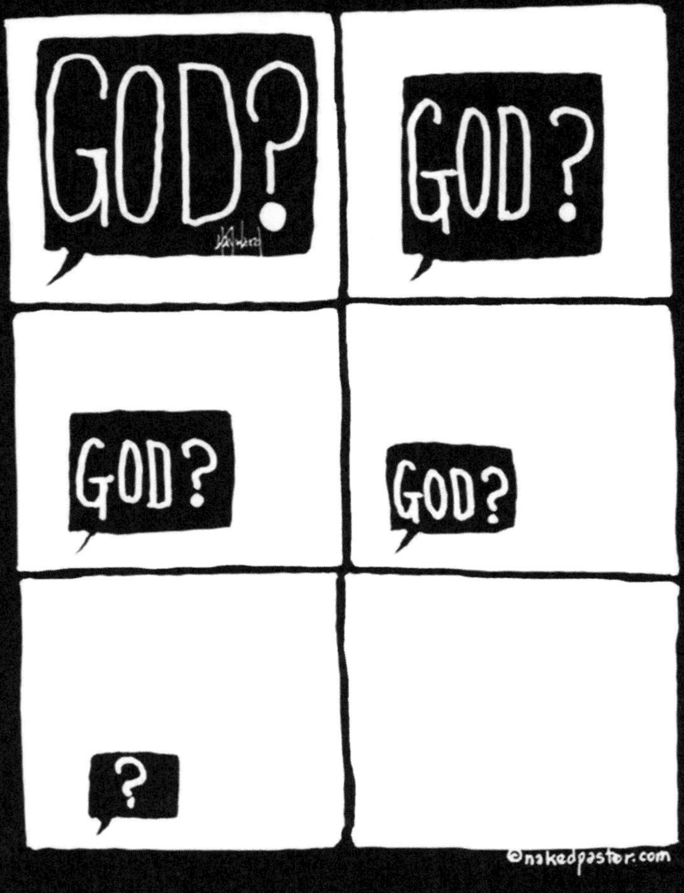
GOD?
GOD?
GOD?
GOD?
?
©nakedpastor.com

remember the first prayer I ever learned:

> Now I lay me down to sleep
> I pray the Lord my soul to keep. And if I die before I wake,
> I pray the Lord my soul to take.

I have no doubt this prayer has been frightening children of all ages since its 18th-century origins. It certainly caused me many an anxious night as I tried to fall asleep without imagining my probable death a few hours later. As I fidgeted in bed, the questions would arise: I could die in my sleep? Why would I die in my sleep? Why would God not keep my soul in my body? Did God have control here? Where was he taking it after I died? Since I'm praying for him to take it, is there a chance he might not? Why might he not take it? What will happen to it if he doesn't? How do I make sure he does? Who else might be dying in their sleep?

As you can see, I struggled with theological issues at an early age. Thanks to this prayer, the thought that I was at the mercy of God's whim became embedded at a very formative age. I learned that to stay on the good side of God's whim, I needed to pray. So I prayed—a lot. I prayed when I woke up, when I went to bed, before every meal, before exams, before traveling, when I was sick, when I was healthy, when I needed something, when I got something, when I lost something, when I found something, when I forgot something, when I remembered something. I prayed for people I loved, people I didn't like, even people I didn't know. I prayed when there wasn't anything in particular to pray about. I prayed especially hard right after I did something that was "sinful in God's eyes" that the ground wouldn't open up and swallow me whole (Yes, I actually believed it would!). In my underdeveloped mind's eye, the prayers were working—life was pretty good, not to mention I kept waking up every morning.

Then I became a teenager, and the whole system started to fall apart. Like any teen, I became increasingly distracted by friends, especially friends of the female persuasion. My time-allocation faculties and event-prioritizing abilities became severely affected by the sudden and abundant influx of hormones coursing through my veins. Since I decided to spend more time talking to girls, or at least coming up with elaborate schemes to get to a point where I could talk to girls (okay, yes, that was how most of the time was spent), something else had to give.

That something was schoolwork, and my grades started to slide. *Slide* might be an understatement. Perhaps *plummet* would be more accurate. You would think I'd be smart enough to see the connection, but apparently my common-sense barometer was also malfunctioning. My solution? Pray harder. In the past, I had prayed for academic success and received it, so now that the work was becoming more difficult, I just needed to pray about it more earnestly, and more often. Right? We all know how this ends: I would quickly discover that all the praying in the world wasn't going to make up for my lack of studying, to the point that I flunked and had to repeat a year of school. Not my finest moment.

It was becoming abundantly clear that there was more of a connection between my efforts and a desired outcome than prayer. So at the risk of putting myself on God's naughty list, I experimented with not praying. It wasn't as easy as I thought it would be for a couple reasons. I was trying to rid myself of an ingrained habit based on an embedded theological perspective. I had a new appreciation for how difficult it must have been to turn the *Titanic* away from the iceberg.

I was also spending a lot of time in church. It was the center of both my spiritual and social lives. At that time I was allowed to go to three places: home, school and church. I had one home, one school, but I wasn't limited to one church. I began hanging out with friends at their churches. I began playing keyboards for another youth choir in addition to being a regular musician at my own church. On any given Saturday night, there was a church somewhere having a choir concert with no less than a dozen choirs from other churches. The next week, it might be a different venue, with many of the same choirs. Barbados is an extremely small island, and there weren't many choirs to go around. So between rehearsals, performances and anywhere from one to three Sunday services, there wasn't a whole lot of time I wasn't in church.

It was a highly evangelical experience. Lots of out loud (emphasis on the *loud*) praying and praising and worshiping and waving and singing and swaying. There were also lots of eyes watching to see if I was doing all the praying and praising and worshiping and waving and singing and swaying that I was evidently required to do, or there would be questions later. So I learned to "pray" without praying. One part of my brain went into autopilot to lead my body through the motions, while the other half was completely focused on something else. If it had been my schoolwork, I would've stood half a chance, but alas, it was girls.

It was a highly schizophrenic time. I felt very conflicted. I very briefly entertained the thought of not going to church—maybe for a nanosecond. I knew if I decided to leave the church, it wasn't the wrath of God I would have to worry about. Hell hath no fury like three generations of strong, loud Christian women who believed it was God's way or no way, and their son/nephew/grandson was going to church! So my experiment continued. I put on a good show in public and ceased praying in private. As far as I could tell, not praying made no difference. I still woke up every morning. I still had mostly good days. I still clashed with my parents. I still lost things. I still found things. I still traveled safely. I still got sick. I still got better. Both wonderful and heartbreaking things happened to the people I loved and the people I didn't like. Did I lose my faith? Maybe not entirely, but I know I was losing my faith in prayer. By the time I moved to the United States for college, it was pretty much gone.

For the first couple years, I still put on a good show as a believer, holding strong to his faith. It was all I knew how to do, and I did it well. I was "that guy"—you know, the guy walking around campus wearing the Top-10-Reasons-God-Is-Like-Coca-Cola T-shirt who sang in the gospel choir and was a member of the student Bible study group. By the way, what is the No. 1 reason God is like Coke? He's the "Real Thing." Yes, I was a walking propaganda board. Here's the thing about propaganda: You can only push a message you don't believe in for so long.

Two pivotal events happened at about the same time that let me finally give myself permission to drop the charade. The family members I was living with moved away, and for the first time in my life, I was truly on my own. Only after they moved did I admit to myself that I was also keeping up appearances for them, and although they didn't care one way or the other, they were reporting back home. I was also enrolled in an elective course called "The Life of Jesus." Did I neglect to mention I was attending a Methodist college? This class exposed me to some of the realities of the Bible for the first time, such as the fact that none of the authors of the Gospels were alive during the time of Jesus; that some of those same authors put words into Jesus' mouth; that some of Paul's letters weren't written by Paul; that much was lost in translation and misunderstood outside the context of a first-century occupied nation; that politics played a large part of the construction of the Bible. It was the final straw. I was done with God. It was a textbook crisis of faith. I saw it, however, as freedom. For the next two years, I lost myself in the fullness of the college experience. And that's all I'll say about that—no need to share the gory details.

Seven is a particularly mystical number. It's a number of perfection. There are seven days in the week, seven colors of the rainbow, seven notes in a musical scale, seven wonders of the ancient world, seven original liberal arts, seven continents, seven days of Kwanzaa, Seven Valleys of the Baha'i Faith, Seven S's of the Nowruz (Iranian New Year), Seven Fruits (Afghanistan New Year), seven deadly sins, seven stars in the Big Dipper, seven pieces in a Tangram puzzle, and let's not forget the Seven Dwarfs. Therefore, it might not have been by accident that I encountered Unity and its principles seven years into my "experiment." What an encounter it was!

During my last few months of college, I was beginning to tire of life without a spiritual anchor, and then I met a girl. Not just any girl—*the* girl. The one who I thought was returning a sense of meaning to my life when, in fact, she was bringing it for the first time. She introduced me to Unity, and while my first thoughts were wondering what bizarre cult I had walked into, my second and third thoughts were, How could I walk fast enough into it to win over this girl? Win her over I did—we got married two years later.

I was also won over, and not just by her. I was enthralled by a new way of experiencing God. It wasn't an easy transition though. There was a plethora of embedded beliefs that needed to be dug up and disposed of, or at least, addressed. For the first time, I began to see myself as an expression of Divine Blessing—not Original Sin. The concept of being created in the image and likeness of God now made sense. I began to gain a deeper understanding of what it meant to have a relationship with God—it was an inward journey of deepening my understanding of myself. Prayer also began to make sense for the first time. By reading the works of great spiritual thinkers, such as Eric Butterworth, I learned that I was to pray *from* God, not *to* God. I learned that my prayers were to be acknowledgments and affirmations of my inherently divine nature, not platitudes to a fickle deity; that my thoughts and words carried the creative power of the universe, no wishful thinking nor soliciting for external intervention.

I started to see that prayers weren't just words. Any action that expressed my divine nature was, in effect, a prayer. When I was in service to others, I was being a prayer. When I was immersed in any experience that let me touch the depth and vastness of what lay beyond what I could perceive with my senses or imagine with my mind, I was in prayer. When I would sit at the piano and let my fingers effortlessly play notes that transported me deep within myself, I was praying.

Music has always had a certain transcendent ability to express what words cannot. The great composers (and artists of all genres) knew this and have always been able to bring the intangibly sacred to the level of perception. One night I glimpsed a deeper understanding of Divine Love as I listened to Al Green's[1] 1971 smash hit "Let's Stay Together."[2] I used to hear the opening lines as a pathetic co-dependent plea, one I once lived from—"I am so in love with you, whatever you want to do, is all right with me." Now I heard those words as a declaration: Together we are standing in relationship from a place of Divine Love, so much so that regardless of your actions, I see the truth of who you are, and I love you anyway, and I love myself enough to know I will be whole. Such an affirmation of relationship has to be a prayer.

What would the world be like, I wonder, if we all lived from such a place? Was this what Jesus meant by "Love your neighbor as you love yourself"? What would he have to say about prayer today? It's anybody's guess, but I suspect he would have little to say and much to show. I imagine he would be devoted to creating experiences for himself and others to experience the absolute boundless Presence of God. Being partial to the creative and expressive power of music, I could see Jesus being a musician, weaving perfectly sublime yet primordial melodies that allow us to eclipse space and time and touch the infinite. Or perhaps a DJ, spinning tracks and dropping grooves that let our minds, bodies and souls become a seamless whole as we coalesce into an elemental Oneness. That would be the ultimate prayer.

2

It's Me, Isn't It?
→ The Question of Self-Awareness ←

IT'S ME, ISN'T IT?

I've made many assumptions in my time. When I board a plane, I assume every other adult on the plane has done so at least once. This is 2012 after all. I didn't consciously know I had made this assumption until a recent flight when I sat across the aisle from a man in his late 30s or early 40s who seemed to be having trouble fastening his seat belt. I thought, Oh, great. It's a full flight, and his belt is broken, which means we'll have to deplane, and I'll probably miss my connecting flight ... The litany of internal complaining continued in my head until he took out the comically colorful pictogram instruction sheet (you know, the one we fan ourselves with before the air comes on) and followed each step successfully. Then it hit me: This is the *first time* this guy is flying! I nudged the obviously veteran-flying, thirty-something couple beside me, and we proceeded to witness the greatest in-flight entertainment in 30 years since the movie *Airplane*!

It was obvious as the plane took off that this guy was not a city slicker, and he was expressing more childhood amazement than any boy ever could. He gripped the seat handles tightly, exclaiming, "Oh, boy ... Woo-hoo!" as we took to the air. It was about a two-hour flight, and after 15 minutes of looking out the window then quickly leafing through everything he could read in the seat pocket, he quickly realized what we all know: Unless we bring our own entertainment, commercial flying is just plain boring. He eventually fidgeted himself to sleep after a trip to the bathroom, which he announced was the skinniest he'd ever seen.

By far the most priceless moment was upon landing. As the plane descended, we could see both his excitement and anxiety levels rise. With about a minute to touchdown, he asked, "Are we fixin' to land?" Upon hearing that we were, he pulled out his cellphone, called a friend, and *narrated the entire bumpy landing*! It went something like this: "Okay, we're gonna land ... here we go ... *Oh, Holy Sh**!* ... pardon my language (to the mom and little girl seated next to him) ... Hooweee, that hurt ... I'll call you back." We were cracking up across the aisle. I doubt the flight attendants would have been laughing since he was bending the rules by using his cell before landing, but they were buckled in and missed the entire episode. It wasn't my finest moment, and I maintain we weren't laughing at him but sharing the childlike joy and excitement of first-time travel he was experiencing. Okay ... we were laughing at him, but it was a truly humorous sight to behold. Again, I'm not proud of my behavior.

To be honest, I am in awe of such people who are so comfortable in their own skin that they are not the least bit concerned how they appear to other people. It takes a certain kind of courage, self-awareness and self-assuredness to pull that off. I wish I was such a person. If I had to grade myself on a scale of one to 10, one being a place of obsessive concern with others' thoughts about me and 10 being the poster child of nonarrogant self-assuredness, I would give myself a six. And that's being generous. I would hazard a guess that the reason I get concerned about what others think is that I'm still not clear about what I think of myself, so I tend to rely on the judgments of others.

IT'S ME, ISN'T IT?

I recently went through what could best be described as a one-third life crisis. Still in my thirties, I was too old for the quarter-life I'm-an-adult-now shock, and too young for a midlife meltdown. But my experience was similar: an awareness that I did not know who I was; the realization that I was playing out my life roles as if they were scripted movie scenes. Interestingly enough, it all started when I had what is commonly referred to as my "Call to Ministry." The moment was not one of shock and awe comparable to finding a burning bush. It was more like a gradual awakening to something I knew all along—I just hadn't known that I knew it. It was like noticing a mailbox on the corner of the street and wondering out loud when it was put there only to have the person next to you look at you as if you just returned from a trip to the Twilight Zone, because it had always been there, and you had been walking past it for years. I wasn't ready to see it until that moment, and I responded with an enthusiastic "Oh, no!" I had seen the behind-the-scenes life of more than one minister, and I didn't want it. Ministers were always on call. Their congregants saw them more than their family did. They were overworked, underpaid and were always expected to be in a state of humbled bliss. This was not the life I had imagined for myself. Well, I had a choice, didn't I? Who said I had to answer this call?

Up to this point in my life, I had imagined that I understood the Bible story of Jonah. Briefly, God asked the prophet Jonah to go preach to the citizens of a town called Nineveh. *Preach* might be understating it—Jonah was instructed to tell them that God's wrath was on its way. Jonah, probably thinking they might kill the messenger, decided to run as far as he could from Nineveh. He finds passage aboard a ship, but soon after setting sail, a storm threatens to sink them. Jonah believes God's anger has caught up with him, so he tells the men on the boat to throw him overboard. Maritime laws being what they were back then, as in "do what it takes to keep the boat afloat," the men throw Jonah to his doom. But he is rescued, sort of, by a big fish that swallows him whole. The Bible never calls it a whale, but since it had to be big enough to swallow a man, the moniker stuck. Jonah spent three undoubtedly gross and slimy days in the fish before coming to his senses and deciding to follow God's commission. Either that or he'd had enough of the gross and slimy whale guts. The fish vomits Jonah up on the beach (more gross and slimy), and he goes on to lead the people of Nineveh to repentance, ultimately deterring God's wrath.[3]

There is intellectual understanding, and then there is what happens beyond it; a soul-level comprehension beyond words and feelings ... a spiritual understanding, if you will. Because I had an intellectual understanding of Jonah's story, I knew running was futile. Because I had never run from God before, I thought I'd try anyway. And like Jonah, my stubbornness demanded that I have a taste of hell to appreciate the journey of heaven that was to follow. Fortunately, it was not gross and slimy.

I was a music teacher in an inner city charter school at the time. It was a pressure cooker of stress. I never wanted to be a music teacher. My undergraduate degree was in music therapy,[4] and I loved being a music therapist, especially one who had his own private practice, set his own hours, answered to no one. But we had relocated so my wife could attend the same seminary I was hell-bent on avoiding. She was a full-time student; I had to feed my family. This was the only job I could find. I told myself I could do anything for two or three years to get Jennifer through school, and then we would go wherever she was called to minister.

For the first time in my life, I got up almost every day to do something I was not passionate about. I quickly figured out I wasn't built for that. I had a newfound admiration and incredulity for people I knew who had been in jobs they hated for decades, and this was only after one semester. Music therapy was about regaining life through music. Music education, as I saw it, was about imparting knowledge. I'm not knocking the profession; one of my dearest, most influential role models was a music teacher.[5] But it was not where my heart lay. Middle and high school students are challenging enough; teaching them in a city adds another level of demand and difficulty. I was often overwhelmed with their needs and behaviors, with the apathy and hostility. This was also a college preparatory charter school, so there was the added pressure on the students to perform academically. It didn't help that we had longer days and longer semesters than the average school. Music, while appreciated, was not a priority for the administration. This was apparent when one year my eighth grade classes were turned into extra/remedial math sessions ... and I was required to teach them!

It wasn't all bad. I witnessed the tenacity of some students determined to use this opportunity to succeed. I worked with some amazing musical talents that I'm certain will take the world by storm someday. Yet after three years, I was burned out. I knew it was time to quit when it took most of what I had in me to get out of bed and get in the shower. Then I had to talk myself into getting into the car and driving to work. When I got to work, I would sit in the parking lot, mustering the last ounce of willpower to get out of the car and through the doors of what felt like a life sentence. I should make it clear that this was my issue. I'm not speaking against the school or administration. I have nothing but sheer admiration for public school teachers who love to teach, are good at teaching, and are answering their soul's call to teach. I was not one of them.

As a teacher whose subject wasn't under constant scrutiny and evaluation by the state, I was sometimes asked to supervise clubs and extracurricular activities, most of them not related to music. One of them was the National Outdoor Leadership School (NOLS). NOLS provided students with the opportunity to learn leadership and life skills in the great outdoors. They also provided deals for faculty sponsors as well. Now you have to understand something: My idea of roughing it is staying at a Holiday Inn Express with no Wi-Fi. So signing up for an almost two-week camping expedition in the mountains outside Lander, Wyoming, took everyone by surprise, including me. But this was a supervised experience by a nationally recognized organization. It sounded like an easy escape for a couple weeks. Turns out I'm not always right.

The trip started well enough. On the first day in Lander, my fellow faculty campmates and I met our guides (let's call them Bill and Bob), were given a safety tutorial, and were outfitted with the equipment we would need for the trip. It was a pack-supported trip, which meant that a few times during the two weeks, a rider with a fully loaded packhorse would meet us with new supplies. That way all we needed to carry was a backpack with parts for tents, cooking equipment, enough food for three or four days, and our personal items—about 40 pounds. The heaviest thing I'd carried in my life so far was a guitar.

We set off the next day. We were a motley crew, from seasoned campers to first-timers; from students in their 20s to a freshly divorced middle-aged man. We all bonded quickly as we were all excited to be on this adventure. On the first day, we climbed about 1,000 feet straight up the side of a mountain. The idea was to do the hard climbing at the beginning of the trip when we had fresh legs. On the second day we climbed almost another 1,000 feet. By this time we were at an elevation of about 11,000 feet. When we camped for the night, I noticed that my heart rate never slowed down, and I slept no better. Our pace slowed on the third day, but I noticed I could walk only so fast no matter how much I willed my legs to do otherwise. I was in a constant haze.

We would have attributed it to normal altitude sickness, except for a racing heartbeat that kept getting faster, and the odd sensation that with every breath, I was blowing bubbles in my lungs. The next day I could barely walk at a regular pace and had to stop every 15 minutes to rest. The items in my pack were divided between the others because carrying any weight was out of the question. I felt like a burden. Not only was I slowing the group down, but now they were carrying more than their share. I was ashamed of my condition and felt humiliated by what I was sure the others were thinking of me behind their concerned words and kind deeds.

By that evening my walking had deteriorated to a slow shuffle, my breathing to ragged gasping, my mental clarity like that of a dirt-filmed window. The group was split into two. Most of the others went ahead with Bob to set up camp at the appointed location while Bill and one other camper (Ryan, for this story) stayed to walk with me. As dusk approached, it was obvious we weren't going to make it to the campsite. A storm was fast approaching, and since the equipment was divided among various packs, all we had were stakes and a tent cover—no tent, no tent pole. Because of my mental fog, I am still unclear about many of the details of that night, but a few images remained: like losing my balance and almost going over the edge of a ravine only to be saved by Ryan's quick thinking and reflexes; like Bill holding me up and checking my urine stream by flashlight to make sure I wasn't dehydrated ("Clear and Copious" is a catchphrase I won't soon forget!); like both of them sleeping on either side of me with the cover thrown over us as massive drops of rain pelted us. When we finally caught up with the others the following morning, Bill and Bob decided it was time to get me off the mountain. It was Day Five of what was supposed to be an 11-day adventure.

As I sat in the sun struggling to breathe, I realized I had just experienced three tortuous days. What is it about three days anyway? Is that how long it takes God to prove her point? Jonah was in the fish for three days. Jesus rose from the dead on the third day (so technically he was only down for two, less if you take into account he was killed Friday evening, but I'm digressing, and for the mystical purpose of my tale, we're sticking with three). I was ready to admit I was running from my calling to ministry and please get me off that mountain. Which they did, on the back of a packhorse, and if you think normal riding saddles are uncomfortable, your backside hasn't felt anything yet! I was admitted to the hospital, pumped full of oxygen, and diagnosed with High Altitude Pulmonary Edema (HAPE). The doctor was a little befuddled considering HAPE was something climbers trying to scale the big mountains like, say, Everest, might experience.

When I told him I was originally from Barbados, the highest altitude I had lived in was Kansas City, and the only time I had been at 11,000 feet was in a pressurized airplane cabin, his confusion evaporated. I was on a flight home the next day.

You would think I was grateful, but the way I saw it, I was returning to a life I no longer wanted to live. As the plane flew east, my anger traveled north. I was fairly furious by the time I landed. In hindsight, there might have been shades of Post-Traumatic Stress Disorder at work, and I know I was livid at my inability to simply quit my job the next day. I felt stuck, and I misguidedly directed all my anger at the one person who deserved it the least: my wife. Jennifer, who was so relieved to have me home, was blindsided by my naked hostility. Even I did not know where it was coming from, but looking back, I can admit it was years of unexpressed frustrations and needs finally being let loose.

It was the beginning of a realization that I had lost myself, and I didn't know where to find me. For years I had bought into the roles I was playing with such finality that I had forgotten they were just that ... roles. I would tell myself, Here's what a good husband or father or teacher or friend would do, all the while slowly muting the authentic voice that would say, "But this is not who you are."

I began to question every major decision I had made. And thus began three years of deconstruction and rediscovery. What's up with the threes again? During that time, there were many dark nights of the soul, and a few dark fortnights as well. I started seminary with only the inner compulsion that it was mine to do, and with no rational reasoning to back it up. It was a leap of faith that would have one of those Wile E. Coyote[6] moments of midair suspension before I plummeted into a spiritual crisis the likes of which I was not remotely prepared for. Because my sense of self had already been shattered, I was standing only on my faith, and when that rug was pulled out from under me, there was the vast emptiness of uncertainty.

I would later joke that one shouldn't go through a spiritual and personal crisis at the same time ... one is plenty. But as I learned, the two cannot be separated. My spiritual identity is my sense of self. Whether I call myself a believer in something, an agnostic, an atheist, or a member of the spiritual-not-religious sect, my understanding of God is at my core. It was in the emptiness that I found Grace. Not in the traditional sense of God's favor, but in the comfort of eventually finding a soft place to land.

Like a tender seed blown haphazardly by unpredictable winds, I would beyond all odds fall into the fertile soil of unconditional love and support tended by my family, classmates, professors, mentors and friends. I let myself be absorbed into that personification of God's grace, and take root, eventually shooting out a new life ... my own personal understanding and connection and relationship with my Divinity that stretched beyond any dogmas or beliefs, even the ones I was absorbing in seminary. At the time it seemed antithetical to the reasoning behind seminary. Was I not there to deepen my ministerial skills and beliefs in the context of this specific spiritual movement? Yes, and I had arrived at the fork in the path that everyone in seminary, and often in life, comes to: Will my new belief system allow me to continue existing where I am? Could I be a Unity minister and still remain true to who I had become?

This is a crossroads we all face in the course of transformation. The mold into which we once fit, or the roles we once played, may no longer fit the new us. With any luck, we will be surrounded by a loving and supportive cast who will stand by us and adapt to us, acknowledging that transformation is an equal opportunity disruptor/enhancer, and they may want us to do the same for them someday. But there will be some folks for whom you no longer fit into their paradigm.

The reverse will hold true as well. There may be painful separations, wounded hearts, resentments held. The truth is there is no greater injustice we can do to ourselves than not being ourselves. Through it all, however, there will be Grace. In time, there will be a soft place to land.

3

God Wants Me to Do *What?*

→ The Question of God's Will ←

In the history of religion, perhaps nothing has caused as much confusion, oppression and tyranny as the varied interpretations of two words: God's Will. "It is God's Will that (fill in the blank)" is a phrase that has been brandished as the banner of authority by those who claim to speak for God. It was supposedly "God's Will" that during the Middle Ages as many as 200,000 people died in battle because of Crusades.[7] It was "God's Will" that led to two Inquisitions (Medieval and Spanish), resulting in the death of thousands, mostly women accused of practicing witchcraft and burned at the stake. Within the past century, Adolf Hitler, the Ku Klux Klan, and the Islamic extremists responsible for 9/11 all believed they were carrying out some variation of "God's Will."

To be fair, some good has come from it as well. Many have emulated the compassionate works of Jesus and resonated with his edict to love God and love our neighbor. Saints such as Francis of Assisi and Mother Teresa of Calcutta lived out their idea of God's Will by being in service to the poorest of the poor. I'm clear that in my early teens, living out my understanding of "God's Will" kept me out of trouble. During these years, others were telling me "God's Will" as a code for living my life, which, although presented with inspiring words like *prosper* and *birthright*, seemed to involve a long list of things I shouldn't be doing, which, unfortunately, I was by my early twenties.

Paradoxically, and problematically, both the dilemma and the solution of "God's Will" lie in our understanding of God. Who can understand God? Well, perhaps we all can, but only in our own way, not all at once, and certainly not the totality of all that is God. To compound this, our understanding of God will evolve as we evolve. Years ago, when my understanding of God shifted from the loving-yet-vengeful-so-better-fear-Him-puppet-master-in-the-sky to the underlying essence of all there is, the term *God's Will* lost meaning for me. I no longer thought of God as a person, but as Principle. People have wills and desires and needs, not principles. How could a principle have a will? Does Gravity have a will? No, Gravity just does what it does. It is not subject to emotional tantrums, deciding to punish us when we attempt to deny it by withholding its very nature and flinging us off into the cold, dark depths of outer space. Could you imagine every time we jumped or an airplane took off, Gravity suspended or reversed its pull out of spite?

To some, "God's Will" had also become a catch-all to attempt explanation where one was not readily, and would never be, available: The sudden death of a young and healthy loved one; a natural disaster that destroys the lives of thousands; an incurable disease. In New Thought movements such as Unity, the term "God's Will" shouldn't have traction, but it does. It's often, and mistakenly, referred to as "Divine Order." I hear "It's in Divine Order" repeatedly used in many different situations: Someone said it after getting the new job he/she was hoping and praying for; others said it when things weren't going their way; I've even heard it used when someone became seriously ill, and again when they got better. "God's Will" seemed to become a rewording of "I'm not in control here!"

One of Unity's tenets purports that we create our experience through the thoughts we hold on to. While I know this to be true, I don't believe we are individually responsible for every single minute and gargantuan occurrence in our lives. It is irresponsible to believe we are the cause of all disastrous and heartbreaking events, and to imply that another cognizant being is enforcing some cosmic script is equally preposterous.

Despite all this, I realized the term *God's Will* was so embedded in my consciousness that I could not easily release it. To try to eliminate it from my consciousness made me feel like I was trying to remove myself from one of my own core beliefs: I am part of something bigger than myself. So I chose to give it new meaning. I also reluctantly had to admit that I had thrown out the baby with the bath water when it came to the personal relationship idea of God. As the metaphysician H. Emilie Cady pointed out in *Lessons in Truth*, "God may be Principle, but becomes Personal at the point of me ... and you." My reimagining of "God's Will" was an attempt to safely and slowly invite a personal relationship with God back into my life.

So after much time in the question, here's what emerged from the depths of the Silence. Before I share, however, let me be clear that I am *not* claiming to speak for God ... merely for myself. And who am I? Simply an expression of a Divine Principle, which is no small undertaking by any means; at last count there are more than 7 billion expressions running around ... and that's just people! While I don't subscribe to predestination or some master blueprint that is playing itself out, I do believe each of us has a peak optimization of our expression beyond any others. For each of us, there is something that allows us to connect with and express as God in a way that is pure bliss, and others feel it when we're living from and in it. For some it is playing a sport, for others writing, or painting, or preaching, or teaching, or healing ... the list is endless. When we discover and live from a place of unabashed authenticity so that others are inspired and empowered, that, my friends, is God's Will. To put it more succinctly, God's Will is the actualization of my true and authentic nature. I think I can do even better: God's Will is my Authentic Actualization.

My daughter, Joy, is an amazing dancer. She is also a pretty good soccer player. Not too long ago, we were all having trouble keeping up with her schedule of dance rehearsals and performances and soccer practices and games. We asked her to make a choice, and she struggled with it for a few weeks. One day I picked her up from a particularly intense rehearsal for her studio's annual summer showcase. She jumped into the car and stated, without provocation and with absolute clarity like I'd never heard from a 10-year-old, "I don't know what we're going to do about soccer, but I am *not* giving up dance!" Although momentarily stunned by her fervent proclamation, I was not entirely surprised. I knew she loved to dance, but I would not truly understand that she was authentically in her passion until I saw one of her numbers in the summer showcase. The graduating high school seniors were paired with a younger dancer for this elegantly choreographed piece that symbolized a passing of the torch. Each pair of dancers had the stage to themselves for a portion of the piece, and each dancer in the pair had a short solo. Joy called it the "Mini-Me" dance.

I had seen Joy dance countless times and I'd be lying if I said I didn't have more than a little Proud Papa bias, but this time was different. I can't sufficiently convey how I saw her lose herself in her graceful movements for what seemed like an eternity but would turn out to be mere seconds. She held our rapt attention as she moved in the beam of the spotlight, a place she usually avoided. If I had to choose words to tell you how I felt in that moment, the best I could conjure up are *rapture, paralysis, nirvana, breathless, grace, elevation, overwhelm, tears*. Later I would ask her if she remembered that moment in the car, and what she had been working on that day. She did. It was the "Mini-Me" dance.

When we are on purpose and living our bliss, we are expressing God's Will, and it is of our choosing. We're not fulfilling some preordained mandate. The only way we're not expressing God's Will is when we're not living from our authentic selves, when we're living a life of "should," and the only people that might be frustrated with that are us ... remember, Principle doesn't feel. So if you're wondering what is "God's Will" for your life, just ask yourself this: What am I authentically passionate about? The answer you come up with is the only answer you'll ever need.

4

What Century Is This Anyway?
→ The Question of Equality ←

"God, please give me a reason to get up today."

WHAT CENTURY IS THIS ANYWAY?

Sometimes things happen that, for all your logic and intellect, momentarily paralyze you with disbelief. One year my wife, Jen, and I were attending the Unity People's Convention in Kansas City. It is the convergence of Unity ministers, congregants, church vendors, musicians, and not just Unitics, I mean Unity folk, either. People from other New Thought and mainline denominations also make an appearance. About halfway through the convention, Jen said, "I want to tell you something that happened, but I don't want you to get upset." Statements like that aren't usually followed by good news. She attempted to be delicate as she told me about the following (paraphrased) conversation that took place between her (**JEN**), an innocent bystander (**IB**), and a booth attendant (**BA**):

JEN: Did my husband just come by and make a purchase?

BA: No, ma'am. I don't think your husband was here.

JEN: Are you sure? He said he was going to come by about five minutes ago.

BA: I'm fairly sure he wasn't here.

IB: There was a guy here five minutes ago.

BA: That couldn't have been your husband ... he was black.

When Jen recounted this, my brain literally stopped working due to the shock. For a few moments, I couldn't process what I had just heard. As a coping mechanism, I tried disbelief, and even hinted that she must have misheard because it was absolutely impossible that in the 21st century someone assumed that a blond-haired, blue-eyed Caucasian couldn't be married to a black man. Even more bizarre was the fact that this took place at a Unity convention. Unity ... the poster movement for acceptance with a discrimination disclaimer a mile long; a movement where you could have green skin and antennas growing out of your head, and you'd still get some love!

The only way I could rationally comprehend the incident was to believe that, for a brief fatigue-induced moment, this man's embedded worldview got the better of him. I made up a story that because he was a white man in his 60s (perhaps 70s and aging well), and by his accent, he was most likely the product of a wholesome Midwest upbringing that told him people who look different don't get married. Most likely because of life experience and Unity's teachings, he intellectually turned his back on his childhood prejudices to become an equal-opportunity lover of humanity. But in that moment, as in many moments of our lives, he switched to default and spoke without thinking. It was a startling reminder that, a scant generation or two ago, things were indeed different, and yes, we've come a long way.

That episode reminded me of a poignant moment Jen and I experienced only two nights before we got married. We lived in the Washington, D.C., metro area, at the time. We drove to the Reagan National Airport to pick up her best friend from college and maid of honor only to find the flight was delayed. We were given the unexpected gift of two hours of peace during a time of hectic preparations, and rather than return to them, we decided to head over to the nearby National Mall. We soon found ourselves on the steps of the

Lincoln Memorial. Although it was close to midnight, we were not alone: Other lovers were strolling around or cuddling nearby; tourists were snapping pictures of the almost 20-foot tall, white marble statue of the nation's 16th president.

While we sat hand in hand contemplating the events that would soon unfold and the future that lay before us, we were drawn away from our immediate world by a familiar voice reciting well-known words. The easily recognizable intonations of Martin Luther King Jr. floated through the air, delivering what would become a defining moment in the American Civil Rights Movement: the "I Have a Dream" speech. We searched for the explanation of this surreal moment and saw a group of high school students sitting on the steps diagonally above us. In front of them was a man who looked like he was reenacting John Cusack's boom box scene from the movie *Say Anything*. He slowly paced back and forth to the rapt attention of the teenagers, boom box held high over his head, the words of that enduring address streaming out full blast. We joined the outskirts of the group, moved by the historical significance of that moment not long ago on the steps we were sitting.

We became all too aware that, not long ago, it would have been illegal for us to marry because she was white and I was black.[8] We shuddered with the realization that less than two generations ago, the love we were expressing could have led to at best my imprisonment, at worst a violent death. Being the Truth students we were, we quickly moved to a place of gratitude. We were grateful for a civics teacher that would bring history alive for his students from California and remind them that their freedoms were hard-fought and shouldn't be taken for granted. We were grateful we were born and lived in the times we did, that the law was now on our side, and we were free to stand before friends and family to be joined as husband and wife two days later.

Let's fast forward 13 years. While remnants of racism still linger, laws have been established to ensure that overt discrimination based on an individual's skin color or ethnicity will not be tolerated. The same goes for gender. Women are equals and entitled by law to every right afforded a man (Full disclosure: After seeing my wife give birth, I give the edge to women!). Officially, racism and sexism are no longer an issue. The current issue, however, is sexual orientation, especially the right for same-sex couples to marry. It is appalling that it even is an issue given this nation's recent history of discriminatory behavior. The difference, however, is that some are convinced that sexual orientation is a moral issue, and sadly, they use the Bible to support their view.

Discrimination of all kinds is continually perpetrated and defended by those who simply refuse to evolve in their thinking about what is written in the Bible and other Holy scriptures. I marvel at black ministers who use isolated Bible passages to rationalize their opposition to homosexuality and legalizing gay marriage. Did they conveniently forget the same Bible was once used to justify the horrors of slavery? Women who speak out against homosexuality as an ungodly act also seem to have overlooked the fact that women were viewed in the Bible as property, on par with livestock and land. I am baffled that many of these same women willingly belong to faith movements that treat them as less than equals under the disempowering theology of "complementarianism." This archaic view would say that although essentially equal, men and women have different but complementary roles. Sounds good on paper, right? Yet somehow none of the leadership and decision-making roles are ever assigned to women. They get to "collaborate with" and "support" their husbands, and are denied other rights, such as being ordained as ministers in some movements. "Equal but Complementary" doesn't sound too far from "Separate but Equal." Just sayin'.

I digress, and perhaps judge too harshly. How anyone chooses to express their understanding of God is their human and constitutional right. Speaking of the Constitution, what I don't think is right is the increasingly common practice of states amending their constitution to enforce a belief of inequality. Wasn't this country founded on the idea of freedom of expression ... of religious expression? I'm not from this country, but that's how I understand it. So to create laws that would support the disenfranchisement of any group of people based on religious interpretation seems, well, downright un-American.

Yes, I know I'm probably preaching to the choir here. I have to ask myself, What am I, as a choir member, doing about this? I could say, and have said in the past, that since this isn't a problem in Unity, this isn't a problem. That would be like saying there isn't a hunger or homelessness issue because I live in a house with a stocked refrigerator. Is it enough to say I belong to a movement that accepts all, so I've done my part? Hardly. I get to be in action with my vote when the opportunity arises, with my money by supporting organizations that do support gay marriage, and with my time and energy by marching in protest alongside my friends and family members who do not have the same legal rights afforded to me.

Do I also have a greater responsibility as a minister? Absolutely. That responsibility is to be a loud voice for the other side of the God story that seems to be often and conveniently forgotten. That side is the simply elegant prose of the one upon whose teachings Christianity is founded—Jesus. When asked, "What is the greatest commandment?" His reply was to love God with our heart, soul and mind, and to love our neighbor as ourselves. Depending on where you read this passage, the rebuttal question is, "Yeah? So who's my neighbor then?" (Only maybe a lot less snarky and without the English accent, which I inexplicably just imagined was delivered.) It was a great question that led to one of the most heart-opening call-to-action parables of the New Testament—the Good Samaritan.[9]

In this tale for the ages, Jesus basically called out his fellow Jews by making the hero of the story a Samaritan. Although ancestrally related, the Jews looked down on the Samaritans. So you could imagine their ire when in Jesus' story the victim of a vicious attack and robbery was helped, not by a Jewish priest or a Levite (the upper crust of priests), but by a Samaritan. They didn't see this one coming—Jesus could spin a good yarn.

I think the crowd missed a great opportunity to ask an even more important question: How do I love myself? Because isn't that at the heart of the issue? Before I can love my neighbor, I have to love myself. All love begins with self-love. Unfortunately, the opposite is also true: All loathing begins with self-loathing. So if there is nothing else we are here to do, it is to love ourselves ... with full abandon, as though there was no chance of disappointment, our hearts wide open and streaming rays of compassion to shed light on a shadowy world. Only then will loving God and loving our neighbor be one and the same.

5

Poor Parenting in Progress

→ The Question of Conscious Parenting ←

Dad, I hate to do this to you, but I think I'm gay. I'm just telling you now so you have time to prepare for your theology to be seriously challenged.

POOR PARENTING IN PROGRESS

We might be letting our daughter watch too much TV. Once when she was 10, she overheard Jen and me talking about the shades of depression that sometimes cast a gloomy haze on my outlook on life. The next few exchanges went like this:

Joy: Wait, Daddy's depressed?

Me: No, I don't think so. I just get sad for no reason sometimes, but it never gets so bad I can't handle it. Do you know what depression means?

Joy: Not really, but I know it hurts ... and Cymbalta[10] can help!

Cymbalta was the antidepressant du jour and the commercials were pervasive. Want another example? Joy was bitten on her chest by a tick when she visited the great outdoors, also known as the in-laws' homestead. We pulled it out, but there was still a huge, swollen red bump in the middle of her chest. The conversation went like this:

Jen: That's huge! It's like Chandler!

Me: Ha-Ha-Ha!

Joy: Ha-Ha-Ha!

Me: Why are you laughing? You don't get it!

Joy: Yes, I do—Chandler has three nipples!

Me: You don't get to watch *Friends*[11] anymore.

Our children, pure and simple, are sponges. They see, record and absorb virtually everything that happens around them. While this makes me shudder just to think about it, this is good news. It means that, theoretically, we could radically transform this planet in optimistically three, realistically four, generations. By the time I am a great-grandparent, there could be world peace, an end to famines and homelessness, an egalitarian society the likes of which we have only read about in fantasy novels. How will our children's children's children manage this amazing feat? By being the sponges they naturally are, which means the change begins with us.

Our children know only what they are taught, and to be honest, adults are not always doing a great job of teaching. Some of us teach our children that there will never be enough for everyone, so they have to hold on to what we have. We do this by buying more than we need and hoarding. Some of us teach our children that only the strong survive, so they have to be stronger and more aggressive at all costs. We do this by bullying each other and our children. Some of us teach our children that it is okay to use brute force to get what they want. We do this by hitting them. Some of us teach our children that it is okay to be dishonest to get what they want. We do this by being dishonest with them. Some of us teach our children that it is better to be feared than to be loved. We do this by intimidating them. Some of us teach our children that it is acceptable not to engage the world and connect with others in meaningful ways. We do this by letting them watch hour after hour of TV. Some of us rob our children of their childhood and innocence, forcing them to be adults before they are physically or mentally or emotionally prepared. We do this by exposing them to scenes and sounds and experiences beyond their years. Some of us teach our children that it is right to discriminate against others because of their ethnicity, race, gender, age, sexual orientation, economic status, weight, appearance, religion or politics. We do this by doing it to each other.

Why do some of us teach our children these things? Because it was what we were taught by our parents, and we have not yet unlearned it. When Jen and I witness parents modeling these behaviors for their children, and yes, when we catch ourselves doing them because we are obviously not the perfect parents, we call it Poor Parenting in Progress (PPP). Here are some examples we have encountered.

In 2007 when Joy was in first grade, the school held a mock presidential election to give a hands-on example of how democracy works. The candidates were Sens. John McCain and Barack Obama. At the time, we lived in a Midwest town whose name I won't mention here. We asked Joy who she was going to vote for. She said Barack Obama because she wanted to help elect the first black president of the United States. True confession: Since he was our choice as well, we were happy with her decision and told her she made a wise choice. However, she was extremely distressed when she came home on Election Day. Some of her classmates told her not to vote for Obama because, if he won, he would enforce a ban on Webkinz, those cute stuffed animals with online avatars. Joy loved Webkinz, and while she stood by her vote, she was obviously torn by the potential outcome based on that bit of news. News, I imagine, no child could have concocted alone. Now I'd like to think if Joy had told us she was going to vote for McCain, we would have told her it was her choice. To be fair, we probably would have tried to sway her vote, but I'm confident we wouldn't have used such a dishonest, albeit creatively underhanded, scheme.

I have another, more recent example. In 2011, Joy auditioned for a role in the Carolina Ballet's production of *The Nutcracker*. It was one of the few performances in which the professional studio included children. This was Joy's first time auditioning for this particular production. We had been living in Raleigh for a few years but usually traveled during the Christmas holiday, often to visit my family in Barbados. Yes, I know, what a holiday burden! But truth be told, even a tropical paradise isn't so paradisiacal when all your family is there. We decided not to go so Joy could audition, and she got a part as one of the girls in the opening party scene. Being totally oblivious, we were simply glad she was selected to be in the production. We had no idea what a coup it apparently was to land the part since this wasn't Joy's studio putting on the production. We soon found out. It began with other parents' surprise that on her first audition she was selected to be a Party Girl. It was a part many of the dancers, who had been in previous productions, had aspired to. Other than the lead role of Clara, it was the best part available to the young dancers. It also didn't help that she was selected as one of their stronger dancers to be part of the upcoming spring production of *The Little Mermaid*. But what drove home the high level of the parents' dissatisfaction, and perhaps their childrens', was one of Joy's classmates telling her the only reason she got the part was because she was black!

Joy's response to her classmate was "So what." I told her should that happen again, say, "Yay for Affirmative Action!" (And I sometimes wonder where she gets her sense of humor.) Again, I suspend my belief that a child came to such a conclusion alone.

Despite her bravado, Joy was obviously affected. The gift of that age, or at least of Joy, is a short memory. She and her classmate were chummy soon after. I, however, didn't move on so quickly. While I verbally reassured Joy of her worth as a dancer by virtue of her skill alone, and that her friend's comments were probably more a reflection of her disappointment and those of the adults in her life, I was saddened and angered that here was another generation being taught to see differences as threatening. Why do we pass on such damaging thinking to our children? Perhaps it's because we haven't made peace with our own childhoods and forgiven the wounds inflicted on us.

One of my mentor ministers had a favorite saying: "People are doing the best they know how to do. Otherwise, they would do different." For years, I called bullsh** on that. (Wait ... can I say bullsh**? No? Okay then ... shenanigans.) All I had to do was look at the atrocities in the news for that day as evidence to the contrary. No way were people doing their best and no way could anyone convince me they were. Naturally, I wasn't taking a look at my own life. I wasn't too self-aware at the time, and living in denial of my own need to evolve was much easier. Then I became a parent. Even before my daughter was born, I discovered the only parenting model I had to emulate was my own parents. Take my word for it ... not the parenting style to write books about. (Which, ironically, I'm doing, so Mom and Dad, if you're reading this—and you should be since it's your son's first book—don't be offended ... I will redeem you ... somewhat ... so keep reading.)

My father was an overly self-confident, larger-than-life Bill-Cosby-esque entrepreneur who taught me not to fear failure. He had more business ventures fail than succeed, but that never took the wind out of his sails. My mother was a tireless worker who taught me to embrace the fullness of life. She made us travel. She took photography and cooking and theology classes. She attempted to learn another language. My parents were excellent providers, yet for all the material comforts, I did not lack, I never felt emotionally safe to discover who I was. While my mother firmly believed in my potential, she tried to nurture it by what I'm certain she believed was constructive criticism. I, however, only heard it as what I was doing wrong. My father ushered me into manhood when I was 11 years old by declaring that since I was becoming a man, we would no longer play games and indulge in meaningless fun. While these were in no way on par with the abuses other children suffered, they were damaging enough for an impressionable child who would go through adolescence and young adulthood plagued by self-doubts and an irrational desire to please others.

Should I wonder why my parents chose their particular style of parenting, I need look no further than their parents, who were even less equipped to be effective nurturers. To further redeem my parents, I know that in their own way, they broke their own patterns. My grandparents' paradigm was that children should be seen and not heard. My parents' paradigm was that children could be heard, but they were children and didn't know what they were talking about, so it didn't count for much.

I wanted to be a different parent. So did Jennifer. It wasn't as simple as just doing the opposite of our parents. It was a call to transcend and include; recognizing there were elements and traditions that deserved to be emulated, and some that needed replacing. It was an invitation into Conscious Parenting. As Conscious Parents, we recognize our child is also a spiritual being, and nurturing her soul is as important as providing safety and material comforts. As Conscious Parents, we provide a safe space for our child to have her own voice, develop her own sense of humor, contribute her own opinions, and at the same time, acknowledge that at age 11, she is not ready to make adult choices. As Conscious Parents, we realize the only way to teach our child to become a compassionate, generous, forgiving, honest, loving and aware being is for us to become it first and then authentically model those traits for her. As Conscious Parents, we model healing by forgiving our own parents for what we thought they should have been or should have given us. They were doing their best given the models put before them.

As Conscious Parents, we embrace parenting as a spiritual practice—an opportunity to be called up to our higher selves, riding the currents of the unconditional love of our children along the way. One morning when Joy was 5, she and Jennifer were having a particularly bad start to the day. They were running late, things couldn't be found, breakfast was burned; both tempers were frayed. As they pulled out of the driveway, Joy was having difficulty buckling her seat belt. In a moment of frustration, Jen stopped the car, turned around and roughly snapped the belt closed. When she arrived at the preschool five minutes later, they were both in tears from the overwhelming morning. Jen apologized to Joy and told her they were going to start the day over. When asked if she wanted to say anything, Joy whispered, "The love between us knows what to do." It was a line from one of her children's books, and in that moment, it served as a reminder about what truly mattered—being with each other from a place of love and compassion at all times.

I began to embrace the full magnitude of the love that stems from the parent-child bond in a singular moment when Joy was 7 years old. Neither of us will ever forget that juncture on our relationship. She will randomly remind me of it by asking, "Daddy, do you remember that time you couldn't stop crying?"

We were watching *It's a Wonderful Life*. It was just the two of us. I had seen the movie many times. It wasn't even the first time I'd watched it since Joy was born. But I'm clear it had never been just she and I for the entirety of this cinematic classic. I almost made it through the film when, for some inexplicable reason, at the moment George Bailey awakened to the true value of what he possessed, I was overwhelmed with such profoundly deep joy and love and gratitude for the girl sitting beside me.

My heart truly burst open for the first time in my life, and all I could do was cry. I cried the tears of a wounded boy who might have thought he wasn't loved. I wept with the realization that, with my daughter, I was experiencing true, unconditional love acceptance that only I could ruin by not choosing to receive it. I felt a love so staggeringly vast I almost couldn't endure it. I cried and hugged her, and then I cried some more and hugged her even tighter. Poor Joy didn't know what was happening. "Daddy, you're squeezing too tight!" was all she could squeak after a solid 10 minutes of my mammoth embrace.

I did not want to let her go. I couldn't let her go. I wanted to hold her and cry and feel that love forever.

6

Jesus, Santa and the Flying Spaghetti Monster

→ The Question of Religion ←

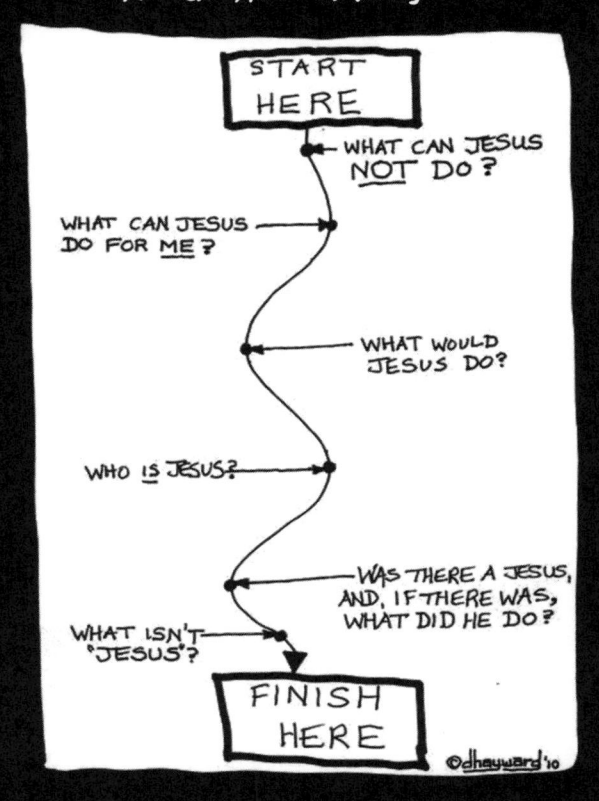

START HERE

- WHAT CAN JESUS NOT DO?
- WHAT CAN JESUS DO FOR ME?
- WHAT WOULD JESUS DO?
- WHO IS JESUS?
- WAS THERE A JESUS, AND, IF THERE WAS, WHAT DID HE DO?
- WHAT ISN'T "JESUS"?

FINISH HERE

©dhayward '10

JESUS, SANTA AND THE FLYING SPAGHETTI MONSTER

Speaking of poor parenting, nothing could be worse than lying to our own children. But we do it anyway, and by "we," I am including myself. Not to pass the buck, but I was forced into the lie, guilt by association, if you will. When Joy was barely old enough to hold her own head up, Jen convinced me that we had to continue the ritual hoax of Santa Claus, closely followed by the fables of the Easter Bunny and the Tooth Fairy. I wanted to tell Joy the truth from the start—these gifts came from your parents, family and friends who paid for them with money they earned by working 40-plus hours a week. Okay, I admit it might be too harsh for a four-month old, but I saw no reason to perpetuate the other option when we knew the truth.

Jen introduced me to other customs that were not part of my childhood: gifts at Easter, and some of the gifts were from us, and some from the Easter Bunny, or from Santa at Christmas. Ours were wrapped and placed under the tree. Santa's gifts didn't appear until Christmas morning, and they were unwrapped, which I would think was odd—he could circumnavigate the planet in one night but couldn't find the time to wrap the gifts? As Joy got older, she discovered other holes in the story. For example, how was the proportioning of gifts determined? Why didn't she receive some things she asked for? Why was a certain gift from Santa and not another? Why did

Santa give her things she didn't ask for and would never use? The more questions she asked, the more lies we would have to tell.

Were we having innocent fun with these mythical creatures? I think not. One morning we were awakened at six o'clock by hysterical crying. Joy was 4 years old and devastated that the Tooth Fairy had forgotten her because the tooth she carefully placed under her pillow the night before was still there. We had fallen asleep and forgotten to make the switch. There was no consoling the poor child until I fashioned a gem of fabrication: "Sweetie, you woke up earlier than usual. The Tooth Fairy just hasn't been here yet!" With a mixture of admiration of my own pure genius and shame from further deceiving my own flesh and blood, I watched the gears in her head turning and the sobbing come to an instant halt as that bit of logic satisfied her. She crawled into our bed and fell asleep, no doubt exhausted from all the caterwauling. While she slept, I snuck into her room and placed two dollars (a little extra for the trauma), further sullying my hands with this crime.

I didn't get presents at Easter when I was a child or money when a tooth fell out (or taken out on one unforgettable occasion involving string and a slamming door). At Christmas, all the presents were wrapped and clearly labeled "To" and "From," so there was no reality confusion. Sad you say? Not as sad as the day a believing child discovers these pillars of her childhood do not exist. Two years ago, in a desperate attempt to make the magic last longer, Joy asked us not to tell her that Santa wasn't real because then she'd have to believe us. I told her she could believe whatever she wanted no matter what I said, but the crestfallen look on her face told me it would be the last year of Santa Claus. Leave it to Jen to prove me wrong, however. She refused to accept the child-to-tween rite of passage, and Santa came again one year ago, along with Joy's knowingly, sympathetically devious smiles. It's clear she has discovered that as long as she keeps "believing," there will be more loot on Christmas morning.

Why do some of us have such nostalgic attachments despite evidence to the contrary? Do they make us feel safer in a chaotic world? Do they remind us of a simpler, more innocent time in our lives? Interestingly, we take the same approach with religion. Regardless of evidence, some of us still cling to the beyond-logic fantastical pieces of it. To be clear, when I say *religion*, I'm referring to the various man-made dogmas, structures and institutions that have been created to help us understand God. While God is at the center of religion, God has nothing to do with it. It's merely our intellect trying to grasp what is clearly beyond the intellect. This goes for all religious denominations and spiritual movements. As the Zen saying goes, they are fingers pointing to the moon. I can almost understand why we might make the finger more important. Sometimes it's a genuinely attractive finger attached to a beautiful and comforting hand, and that moon seems so far away. Merely thinking about the effort it would take to reach it when that hand is within arms' reach is excruciating. So we become enthralled by the finger.

It's no different than a child becoming enthralled by Santa Claus, who has much in common with Christianity's central figure, Jesus. Here we have two men, who, by all historical accounts, truly existed. Jesus was a first-century Jewish rabbi who would have gone by the name Yeshua when he was alive. Santa Claus was inspired by the fourth-century Greek Christian bishop of Myra, St. Nicholas. They were both generous. Jesus was known for associating with, and healing, the poor and disenfranchised. He was also known for his food multiplication miracles. St. Nicholas also has a few food miracles associated with him, as well as giving money to the poor. In one such tale, he couldn't find an open window to throw in the small sack of gold coins, his usual modus operandi, so he dropped it down the chimney, and it conveniently fell into a stocking that was drying by the fireplace. Sounds vaguely familiar, doesn't it? They both had a penchant for working in secret. St. Nicholas was known for putting coins in shoes left out for him overnight. Jesus repeatedly told the people he healed not to tell anyone, which was somewhat bizarre since I'm certain a blind man who suddenly had restored sight wasn't going to go around unnoticed.

Both Jesus and Santa had followers named Peter. In Jesus' case, it was the disciple upon whom Jesus supposedly conferred leadership of the movement that would follow. In Dutch folklore, St. Nicholas evolved into Sinterklaas, and he had a dark-skinned servant named Zwarte Piet, or Black Peter, whose skin color has been the subject of much debate. He was a Moor in one legend (from Northern Africa). In another, his face was black because he was originally a soot-covered chimney sweep. In yet another tale, he was a slave freed by the Saint, and he served Nicholas by choice. It was Peter's job to carry the book of names. The nice children would get presents from Sinterklaas. The naughty children would get kidnapped by Black Peter and taken back to Spain. And we thought coal in the stocking was a raw deal!

On the down side, both Jesus and Santa might have been a little racially insensitive. I think the Black Peter story speaks for itself. In the Gospel of Matthew (15:21-28), we find a story about a Canaanite woman who begs Jesus to heal her demon-possessed daughter. Jesus first denies her wish, but she does not give up so easily. Jesus is impressed by her persistence and declares the daughter healed. The story is often cited as a testament of the woman's faith and the importance of faith in one's spiritual life. But it was Jesus' initial rebuke that was so startling and out of character for a man who would become the standard bearer of compassion. He said, "It is not fair to take the children's food and throw it to the dogs." At that time, the Hebrews looked down their noses at the neighboring Canaanites, although they shared a common ancestry. Jesus apparently did his part to continue the discrimination. In a well-played one-upmanship (or in this case "one-upwomanship"), the mother replied that even dogs get crumbs from the table. This is an excellent citation of the trickle-down theory[12] if I've ever heard one.

Both Jesus and Santa are central to the Christmas season. Jesus could be said to represent the spiritual aspects of the season since it's his birth being celebrated. Santa, although inspired by a Christian bishop, has come to symbolize the secular and commercial sides of the holiday. Both men lived relatively obscure lives and became legendary postmortem figures. While only one has a major world religion credited to him, they both only require innocent childlike faith in their respective messages.

On average, in the United States, fewer and fewer people are attending church.[13] Is anyone surprised? Christianity's central figure isn't much different than Santa Claus! Religion is truly people's ideas about God taken too seriously. There isn't anything that should be taken too seriously. Visit the "About" page of *www.venganza.org* for another example of how religion is simply a creative endeavor (yes, do it now, then come back ... I'm not going anywhere). That might have been shocking to some of you, silly to others, sacrilegious to yet even more. It illustrates that we too often get too caught up in creed and canon until they become the God we worship.

As a young minister, I'm often asked by other well-meaning ministers and church boards what they can do to get more young adults to attend. I tell them there is probably nothing they can do, but telling the whole truth is a good start. The truth is the only religion that matters is one's own. God should be experienced however one understands and perceives God, whether it is nature, music, energy, love, nothing, everything. While there is unmistakable value in connecting with others of similar thinking and beliefs, it shouldn't be required. Ministers should be like the medical researchers trying to find cures to the incurable diseases of the world—they are working to make themselves obsolete. Ministers should not be about the business of filling pews, but rather emptying them. They ... We ... should have only one task: empowering those before us to seek and connect with their own inner wisdom. In the depth of their own consciousness, they will find the God they are seeking, and they don't need a belief system other than in themselves.

7

Loving and Letting Go
→ The Question of Nonattachment ←

LOVING AND LETTING GO

As humans, we are pretty much at the top of the evolutionary chain. With all the associated gains, however, we suffer more than a few shortcomings. For example, we love to hold on to our stuff. Even when we feel bad about all the stuff we have, we find it excruciatingly difficult to get rid of it or at least to downsize. Every time our family moves, we find ourselves with at least a dozen boxes of things we moved with from the move before, and we still don't know why we're carting them around. In our latest move early this year, I unpacked a collection of VCR tapes. *VCR tapes*?! This is the era of DVRs and Netflix. So why am I still lugging around VCRs? I didn't even set up the VCR player because we hadn't used it for who knows how long. And *still* the tapes made it to the shelf. Do I enjoy looking at the covers that much?

Shame-induced hoarding has even gone digital—TiVo Guilt! Oh, it's a real thing. Google it if you have any doubts. It's the feeling of guilt derived from recording more shows on the DVR than you are able to watch. Are you kidding me? Part of me sees my DVR and thinks, Ooooh ... magic box! I'm not that old but I remember a time when you couldn't even record TV shows in the first place! Then the VCR came along and, if you were blessed with the intellect of an astrophysicist, you could program it to record your favorite show. Even though the victims of TiVo guilt are fully aware that they will never catch up with all their saved programming, they often won't delete any of it—it would only make them feel worse.

The sentimental things are worth hanging on to. Two moves ago we decided to leave our piano behind and give it to friends who always wanted one. Their 6-year-old is the second-most amazingly adorable little girl I know, and they had visions of piano lessons and Christmas sing-alongs. I didn't have the heart to tell them that it was probably a pipe dream that would end with a 400-pound plant-and-picture repository. We made some good memories with that cheap, never-stayed-in-tune upright. I wrote some great music on that thing. Jen and I recorded a collection of original songs with it. We had our fair share of sing-alongs with family and friends. It helped me out of the doghouse more than a few times as I serenaded myself back into Jen's good graces. I've used it for venting, processing, sorting out my thoughts, catharting (yes, I just made up that word), and meditating. There'd be times when I was in some kind of mental or emotional vortex and couldn't see a way out. I'd sit, play the first chords that came to me, and an hour later all's right with the world again.

So why did we give it away? We were simply getting tired of hauling the thing around the country. Did I mention the 400 pounds? Ten years, four houses, two states, and one child later, we were just tired of hauling it around. We were also playing it less, and it was becoming the aforementioned plant and picture repository. It was gifted to us by a minister and friend who hauled it to Virginia from the Midwest. We hauled it back to Missouri and figured it didn't need an East Coast sequel. Yes, I used the word "haul" in some form repeatedly because it is a haul—there is nothing easy about moving a piano. Unless you're the professional movers who strap it on a dolly that they strap to themselves and lift it down icy steps in less than five minutes. They did not bend under the weight of the piano or the memories attached to it. I still have the memories. I just don't have the piano. My electronic keyboard is a paltry substitute, but it gets the job done in a pinch.

We don't just hold on to things; we hold on to actions. I don't mean rituals or cultural customs. I'm talking about doing something the same way because it's the way we've always done it. Churches are particularly proficient at this, which is ironic considering Jesus was a model for *not* doing things the way they were always done. We also hold on to beliefs, stubbornly passing them from generation to generation in spite of the evidence that some of them have outlived their usefulness. Discrimination of any kind is a learned behavior. No child comes into this world with an inborn penchant for discriminating against others. It is a learned behavior, most likely modeled by adults whose beliefs were forged by the actions of adults they observed as children themselves. Given the level of interdependence we have come to, we only hurt ourselves when we discriminate against someone because of their fill-in-the-blank.

Letting go is not often easy or simple. It's particularly challenging when it comes to the people we love. Knowing the possibility of relationships ending and the certainty of people dying does not make it any easier when it happens—especially if it happens unexpectedly. I lost my father 15 years ago but not to death, or some unforgivable rift made impassable by time, or male intimacy issues exacerbated by distance. Our relationship was forever altered by a senseless and viciously violent act that resulted in his traumatic brain injury.

While teenage angst has the tendency to distort the memory of one's parents for the worse, I recall my father brandishing humor and charm as weapons of mass affection. Most everyone seemed to love him. He worked harder than anyone I have yet to know ... six, sometimes seven days a week, usually 12 hours or more a day, keeping our family mini-mart (mom-n-pop grocery) in business. He was an entrepreneur, opening at least three other businesses before the injury. Those would fail, so he wasn't perfect, but he certainly wasn't a quitter.

He was a forward thinker, predicting the impact of computer technology. He bought me a Commodore 64 within two years of its creation while we lived on Barbados, an island that was usually 10 years behind any current innovation. He was an eclectic music lover with a deep record collection and an inexplicable fondness for Kenny Rogers, the Bee Gees, and the Village People. Whenever we had "Culture Days" at school to celebrate Independence, I created the music display with his record jackets. He loved to travel. My parents would close the store every August, and we saw how the rest of the world lived. We toured Europe, South America, Canada, and visited relatives far and wide. I owe my global sensibility to those trips, although at the time I desperately wanted to be home with my friends. He didn't practice corporal punishment, but that didn't mean he wasn't a disciplinarian. He was the first person to tell me "Know thyself." When my mother tried to make us vegetarians, he snuck us out for fried pork chops.

One night when I was away at college in Winchester, Virginia, a group of men ambushed my father as he was walking to his car at the close of business. It was late, it was dark, and, although he carried a gun, he was attacked and overpowered. They bludgeoned him within an inch of his life—it would prove to be a personal vendetta as much as it was a robbery. He was in a coma for days, awakening to a time in his mind before we existed. It would be weeks before most of his memory returned, but his distorted personality would remain, and we would all be forever changed.

He became angry, verbally abusive and withdrawn. Where jovial anecdotes once flowed, now streams of profanity spewed forth. His constant presence morphed into disappearing acts. We would not see or hear from him for unbearably long hours, only to have him turn up with absurd treasures like smoked and salted ham hocks. My mother displayed a strength of character the likes of which I did not imagine existed. She endured his undeserved abuse while running the business and raising my younger brother. I languished in guilt because I usually accompanied my father at night before I left for college. Had I been there the outcome might have been different, or I might have laid bleeding beside him.

For the first few years we prayed and clung to the fleeting hope my father's brain would miraculously repair itself. I should say *they* prayed because I wasn't on speaking terms with God right then. But we slowly surrendered to the reality that we had no control over him or his condition. Over time, and with lots of medication, my father's mood softened. We learned to live with who he is, but the man we knew died that night. We see glimpses of his former self, especially when he is around children like my daughter. He always has a gift and a smile for her when we visit. The rest of us? Not so much. Any conversation is all but guaranteed to deteriorate into quarrel. But such is the nature of the beast called traumatic brain injury.

Do we ever truly let go when there is so much emotion involved? It would seem not. Do I no longer feel anger, nostalgia or guilt every time I see the shell of the man that once was? Not entirely. But I feel them to a lesser and lesser degree with each passing year. Letting go, like forgiveness, turns out to be a process, not a product—a journey, not a destination. A journey that can only be made with love. Only with love can we bridge the chasms of hurt that seem impassable. Only with love can we slowly release our grip on the pain and the story that caused it. Only with love can we embrace a wholeness and peace beyond the realities of any situation. Only with love do we "let God" in the letting go.

While we love, we do not ask why, but give thanks. If only for what was, but also for what will be as a result of the time we had. So to my father I am forever grateful ... not just for the travel or the music or the food, but also for the lessons of manhood I was just too young at the time to appreciate: Work hard, play hard, persevere after failure, enjoy the fruits of success, take care of your family, be accountable, and know who you are. In these memories, and in the parent I am today, I continue a legacy.

Thank you, Dad. I still miss you.

8

I Survived Lent and All I Got Was This Lousy Enlightenment

→ The Question of Self-Sacrifice ←

"I don't care WHAT it says! I'm NOT going in there!"

If I'm grateful to Unity for anything, it's the metaphysical spin (I mean "interpretation") that it applies to traditional Christian theology. For any of you leaving traditional Christianity behind like a jilted lover, be warned: You might find Unity to initially be everything you wish you had in your past relationship, but eventually you realize that relationships are a labor of love no matter who is snoring loudly in the bed beside you, keeping you awake when you have that really important meeting first thing in the morning.

Take Lent for example. In many Christian denominations, Lent is the 40-day period leading up to Easter (or for those from the It's-Five-O'clock-Somewhere denomination, the 40-day recovery after the Mardi Gras hangover). It is traditionally a time of preparation through spiritual practices such as prayer, repentance, sacrifice and self-denial (which is no surprise that it's preceded by one of the most grandiose fetes on the planet). It seems like it's the self-denial component that receives most of the attention. People who haven't crossed the threshold of a sacred institution since before the Reagan administration are asking each other what they are giving up for Lent. It is a true crossover phenomenon.

In the crossing over, however, the true intention behind Lent was lost. It became a battle of willpower over minor vices like chocolate or junk food or beer or texting or Facebook, or ... wait ... Okay, I guess for some of us these *are* major vices.

Sometimes we don't realize how attached we are to something unless we're deprived of it. Not that long ago I accidentally left my smartphone at home one night while I was out with friends. I swear I experienced all five stages of grief[14] in those few hours:

Denial: "I can't believe I left my phone at home!"

Anger: "No, I didn't see his tweet or check-in! I don't have my phone! Why are you all laughing?"

Bargaining: "Please, please, let me hold your phone for a few minutes. I just need to touch one. I can log in to my sites from your browser. I'll give it back ... I promise!"

Depression: "Just ignore me. Don't let my mood ruin the evening. I'm not having fun anyway."

Acceptance: "Okay. The phone's not here. I can get it when I get back home. It's only one more hour. Wait ... why's the room spinning?"

Fortunately, by taking a metaphysical approach to Lent, we can recapture some of its original purpose: a time for spiritual renewal and transformation. Transformation of any kind begins in our minds, more specifically with our thinking. In Unity, Lent is an opportunity to pay attention to the negative thoughts that run amok in our heads, and to release the ones that no longer serve us. Hence the handy LENT acronym: Let's Eliminate Negative Thinking.

While Lent lasts 40 days, the idea of examining and transforming our thinking is a lifelong process. Metaphysically, the number 40 means "as long as it takes." In the Hebrew Bible (aka the Old Testament), Moses and the Israelites wandered in the desert for 40 years, or as long as it took them to get to the Promised Land.[15] In the Christian Bible (aka the New Testament), Jesus fasted in the desert for 40 days or as long as it took him to prepare for the start of his revolutionary ministry.[16]

"As long as it takes" is both good and not-so-good news. I just might alter my behavior in 40 days, but giving up chocolate for that period of time is nothing compared to changing a pattern of thinking that might have existed for 40 years. Is it really about the chocolate or about deriving emotional comfort from food? Is my habit of checking in and sharing my location on Foursquare a fun distraction, or am I attempting to meet a need to be seen because I felt invisible as a child? When I separate myself from the behaviors and observe my reactions, I get a better idea of whether I'm dealing with a casual indulgence or a much deeper issue. So perhaps there is something to the physical deprivation that brings out our awareness to the mental and spiritual elements we need to address.

Both of the earlier references to Moses and Jesus have another common thread: the desert. When we think of the desert, we might envision a dry, hot, dusty, lonely, inhospitable environment. With the possible exception of Las Vegas or a movie set, not many people prefer the desert as a place of residence ... not even temporarily.

Don't worry, I won't recommend it either. But I do encourage taking extended time apart from the routine of life to be alone with your thoughts. That could be a fairly inhospitable environment for some of us! I'm thinking more of a silent retreat—a few days where the only sounds might be the rustle of leaves in the breeze, the trickle of clear water over stones in a stream, the chirping of cicadas at dusk. Under such conditions, we can tune in to the endless chatter in our heads, noticing how much of it is unproductive mind babble instead of positive and affirming gems of self-awareness.

I have received many pearls of wisdom while on silent retreats. Once, while walking through the woods, I kept running into spider webs. I was initially frustrated by the repeated icky feeling of the webs on my face and arms, but then I realized this was a lesson in mindfulness. When I took the time to pay attention, I saw signs that I was about to walk into a web: minuscule leaves floating in midair, suspended water droplets, slender stems bent against gravity's pull or their logical direction of growth. It was a reminder that in life, especially in unfamiliar situations, I don't have to be a victim of the unknown. I can increase my level of awareness and look for the signs that can guide me to the right choices.

Another lesson came during a walk in a light rain, and it was thanks to my raincoat. The humidity at the time was so thick my walk was really a swim, and as I perspired, it became unbearably hot and sticky under the coat. At the time, the rain was barely more than a light drizzle, yet I was becoming soaked from the inside! The very thing that was intended to keep me dry was having the opposite effect by trapping my perspiration, and soon I was dripping with sweat. I weighed my options and took off the jacket, betting that I wouldn't be as wet from the drizzle as from myself, and sure enough, the sweat abated as I cooled. It made me realize how often the things I think will grant me safety and security (a certain amount of money in the bank or a specific job) become a source of great worry and anxiety. Sometimes it's good to have a raincoat, but only if it's doing what it's supposed to. Otherwise, it's time to let it go.

Where is this all leading ... all the fasting and eliminating and silencing? To the ultimate letting go, and possibly where every spiritual practice is pointing toward: the letting go of self and ego and personality until all that is left is the Divine. The Tao Te Ching says, "Reveal your naked self and embrace your original nature!" Just as we remove clothing one layer at a time, our life's work is to progressively remove layers of thoughts and beliefs until one day we stand as we were meant to be, a pure expression of the Divine. We may choose to redress; in fact, we will have to in order to be in the world, but let's remember that while the clothes might make the [hu]man, they aren't the [hu]man.

Move beyond embracing positive thinking and embrace a deeper experience of spiritual practice. As you spend more time in meditation, envision the layers and years of pain, faulty thinking, unempowering beliefs, and even theological constructs falling away. Be brave enough to surrender to the powerful Divine self that lies beneath. Become You.

9

I Am *Awesome!*
→ The Question of Humility ←

I AM *AWESOME*!

One Sunday I gave a talk called "Let Go and Let Go Some More." In the talk, I encouraged listeners to embrace their inherent perfection and work to release the thoughts that kept them from it. My premise for inherent perfection was based on a definition, which states that perfection is to be "entirely without flaws, defects or shortcomings." Sure, I could list many of my flaws and my shortcomings, but then I would also have to admit that these are entirely of my creation, and I apparently strive to maintain them, otherwise they would be gone. I've come to discover that my procrastination, for example, although greatly lessened, was the result of my belief that I was unworthy and inadequate to the task at hand—a belief often contrary to the evidence.

We are perfect at our core, and, with the aid of spiritual principles, our work is to live that state of perfection. It could be a daunting challenge, considering that we sometimes wear our defects as badges of honor, using them as an excuse for forgettable behavior and to evoke sympathy. I shared with the congregation that my 11-year-old daughter embodies a mantra that she never fails to express verbally, and often: "I am *awesome*!" Although it usually goes like this:

Joy: Hey, Daddy!
Me: Yes?
Joy: Guess what?

Me: What?
Joy: I'm *awesome*!
Me: Yes, my dear ... yes, you are.

After the talk someone asked me where the humility was in declaring one's awesomeness. I don't know how other ministers feel, but I love it when I get questions after a talk. It tells me that *someone* was actually listening, thinking, examining their own responses, and in some cases, willing to challenge my opinion, or at the very least, get some clarification. I can be confusing at times. A thought might sound good in my head, but when the words come out of my mouth, it's another situation entirely.

My answer to this congregant was this: The humility lies in realizing that everyone else is awesome as well, and that no one is better than the other. We are swimming in a sea of awesomeness! It's tempting to consider myself further along a spiritual path than someone else because I've been at this longer or I don't get angry as quickly, and therefore, I'm better than them. I am not. Each of us has a path that is unique to us, and there's no one else on it. I can't be further along if I'm the only one on my path.

Any guru out there isn't better than you either. They may be more practiced, but let us not confuse competence with intrinsic worth. Any gurus worth their salt will tell you as much. We are all gurus in our own right. At any age, in any situation, from all walks of life, we have learned from being in the world, and we have wisdom to share. Our greatest teachers are each other.

To that end, please indulge me as I share some of the insights that I have gained from my brief travels around the sun. They are not all original, nor guaranteed to bring enlightenment. They do, however, allow me to embrace myself and the world around me. So in no particular order of importance, I present ...

THE WISDOM OF SWAMI OGUNANDA

1. **Self as I Am, Things as They Are.** I picked up this saying from Donald Rothberg. He is one of the nation's foremost leaders in socially engaged spirituality and author of the popular *The Engaged Spiritual Life: A Buddhist Approach to Transforming Ourselves and the World*.[17] It's a succinct reminder that we are the common factor in all our experiences. The most work we have to do is on ourselves. We can't control the outcome of everything, so it is best to remain nonattached yet not apathetic.

2. **Know Thyself.** This ancient Greek axiom still rings true. All growth begins with self-awareness.

3. **Love Thyself.** It took awhile to get to a place where I could love myself unconditionally, and in full disclosure, I don't do it every day. I should. You should too. All love begins with self-love, and we can only love others to the extent that we love ourselves.

4. **You Are Loved.** And not just by a few people. It's important to remember this when we erroneously believe that we are not worthy of love or acceptance.

5. **Laugh Every Day.** Seriously. Even if it's at something ridiculous, like how I just said "seriously" after "laugh." Be sure to laugh with others, not at them.

6. **Keep Your Heart Open.** Only through being vulnerable can we authentically connect and love fully. I learned this from Dr. Brené Brown, vulnerability researcher and author of works such as *The*

Gifts of Imperfection[18] and *I Thought It Was Just Me (but It Isn't).*[19]

7. **Be Kind.** To yourself and others. Not just with deeds, but with patience, compassion, empathy and love.

8. **Give.** To others and yourself. Give with reckless abandon and with no thought of return. It will feed your soul like nothing else.

9. **Eat Food That Makes You Sigh With Pleasure.** Like bacon-covered flourless dark chocolate cake. Don't knock it until you try it. It's the embodiment of decadence. While intended to be taken literally, it's also about savoring all of life's pleasures. We only get one lifetime (that we're aware of), and it's too short not to enjoy it.

10. **All Things in Balance.** Extremes are the anathema to peaceful living. No good can come from eating too much bacon-covered flourless dark chocolate cake.

11. **Listen to Music.** Lots of music. And then some more after that. Preferably live, almost always loud (depending on the genre). Music should be felt as well as heard. It reaches into us and caresses places beyond the reach of our intellect.

12. **Read Good Books.** Lots of books. Read things outside your comfort zone. Read the classics. Read great fiction and nonfiction. Join a good book club.

13. **Write.** Not necessarily to share or publish, but for process. Writing forces our mind to slow and measure the weight of the words. Writing allows us to separate the forest from the trees. It also gives us a way to look back and see how far we've come.

14. **Cry.** It's so cathartic. I don't know about you, but I never feel worse after a good cry.

15. **Be Still.** Don't do anything. Just be still for a few minutes every day. Meditate. Breathe. This is so challenging in today's world of instant connectivity and breakneck speeds of development. I let technology assist me with the smartphone app equivalent of a Bell of Mindfulness. At random intervals my phone will chime a meditation-bowl-sounding reminder, at which time I pause to close my eyes, take a few deep breaths, and turn my focus within.

16. **Be Grateful.** In a world with an endless bad news cycle, there is no better gift to yourself than to find something to give thanks for. Gratitude is vital to experiencing abundance and prosperity, and I don't mean material riches.

17. **Nap.** Rest (sorry ... not dogs) Is [Hu]man's Best Friend. To "sleep on it" is to recharge and regain perspective. Our mind simply doesn't work right when we're exhausted.

18. **Have Honest Friends.** They will keep you humble when you start to drink too much of your own Kool-Aid. Not that I know anything about that.

19. **Find and Live Your Passion.** It's the only way you will be happy.

20. **Live Your Spirituality.** You might mostly hear "practice your spirituality" but the word *practice* implies a specific time period, or a means to an end, as in "I practice behind the scenes so I can perform as close to perfection as possible in public." Every messy moment is an opportunity for spiritual growth and expression. I prefer my spirituality as a way of being.

Hey, guess what? I am *awesome*! And so are you!

10

Find Your Passion, Find Your Peace

→ The Question of World Peace ←

@nakedpastor

"I think the peace that passes understanding also passed me by."

@dhayward

FIND YOUR PASSION, FIND YOUR PEACE

World peace is like a flying car. We all like the idea of it. We've made movies about it. We might even want it. We're pretty sure it will happen someday. But we have resigned ourselves to the belief that it won't happen in our lifetime. Truth be told, I don't think I want it to happen in my lifetime ... flying cars, that is. Can you imagine the body count? It would be a whole new take on survival of the fittest. World peace, on the other hand, is something I wouldn't mind experiencing before I start claiming Social Security. I don't just mean world peace at the national level, I mean world peace at the inner city street level. Of course, the suburbs too—there's all kinds of behind-the-curtains violence happening in the suburbs.

Now statistics would say that given the world's population increase, we have been killing proportionately less of each other over time, so as a human race we are at least trending toward peace. But complete peace at the macro and micro levels? For some, it's an idea that has reached such fairy tale-like proportions that if there was a representative character, it would have a seat at the roundtable of mythical creatures between Santa Claus and the Easter Bunny.

I, too, used to think it was an impossible goal. Then I happened upon a premise so crazy simple it might just work. You might have picked up on it from the chapter title. I believe we will only experience world peace when we each find inner peace. We will never know blissful inner peace until we are living the life our soul intended us to live. When we are each living from that blissful inner peace, and I mean every human being on the planet, I believe we will no longer have a need to be in conflict with each other. Instead, we will be looking for ways to support each other and help those not living their passion to find it. Wishful thinking? Naïve ideology? Perhaps—yet don't many great movements and inventions begin in the realm of incredulity?

Like most "simple" things, this might not be as easy as it sounds. The path to living our passion can be a difficult one ... if we choose it to be. Or we can let it unfold gracefully and easily. I prefer the latter, and I'll wager you would too. Things started to get easy when I embraced the following principles and used them to guide my daily thoughts and decisions. I call them assumptions because I now simply take it for granted they are true. I can give innumerable real-life examples that support these assumptions and show how much less I struggled after I chose to live from them. If when reading them you find yourself somewhere between mildly bothered or downright outraged, then we're on to something. I invite you to dig deeper and explore why you feel that way. I'm not suggesting you have to take these on as your own, but don't dismiss them without taking the time to investigate your feelings.

1. We already know what is true for us

That knowledge may be buried so deep inside we don't even know where to begin looking. Or it may be screaming so loud that its deafening roar paralyzes us. It might be the white elephant in the room of our consciousness waiting patiently to be noticed while we resolutely ignore it. But it's somewhere inside. If we believe that, it will show up in a form we can befriend. We can choose not to befriend it, but that may only lead to suffering and an unfulfilled life.

2. The Universe is friendly, supportive and abundant

It may not look that way half the time, but looks can be deceiving. You can't judge a book by its cover (insert any illusion-based metaphor of your choice here). We witness atrocities on both a small and grand scale hourly, thanks to the media, Internet and others who can't see the good the world has to offer. However, the vast majority of us can speak to the kindness of strangers, have witnessed the benevolence after natural disasters, and have felt the arms of comfort after personal loss. Many of us can attest to the proverbial opening of one door when another slammed shut in our face.

Einstein said it, so it must be true. Maybe not exactly like that, but he said something along the lines of we can decide if the universe is friendly or not, and our entire lives will be informed by that choice. Okay ... that was a terrible paraphrase. Here is the actual quote:[20]

I think the most important question facing humanity is, "Is the universe a friendly place?" This is the first and most basic question all people must answer for themselves. For if we decide that the universe is an unfriendly place, then we will use our technology, our scientific discoveries and our natural resources to achieve safety and power by creating bigger walls to keep out the unfriendliness and bigger weapons to destroy all that which is unfriendly and I believe that we are getting to a place where technology is powerful enough that we may either completely isolate or destroy ourselves as well in this process. If we decide that the universe is neither friendly nor unfriendly and that God is essentially "playing dice with the universe," then we are simply victims to the random toss of the dice and our lives have no real purpose or meaning. But if we decide that the universe is a friendly place, then we will use our technology, our scientific discoveries and our natural resources to create tools and models for understanding that universe. Because power and safety will come through understanding its workings and its motives.

Some of us, as a result of unfortunate experiences or well-meaning yet misguided instruction, live our lives devoid of trust. It's not only a lonely place to be but a paradigm virtually impossible to maintain if thriving is your goal. We have to depend on others in our life because we cannot survive totally alone.

3. God is real

Or Spirit or Energy Field or Life Force or whatever you wish to call it. There's something that flows in, through and as us. It connects us, literally and figuratively. It is in us, and we are in it, both individually and collectively. It is the creative Principle underlying all that exists. Our lives flow a lot smoother when we're swimming with its current instead of battling upstream against it. It's the feeling in our gut; the small voice in the back of our head; the hindsight we ignored when it was still foresight. We've all felt it. Our resistance to believing it, or the conflicts that arise from naming it, do not negate its existence. It's here, there, everywhere.

I know what the religious historians, skeptics and atheists might say: God is a product of man and that we invented God (and by *God* I'm including all definitions by all religions) as we evolved intellectually and attempted to find answers for life's questions. Some of these questions and answers were deeply profound ("What is the meaning of life?" Not sure that one's been answered yet) while others not so much ("Why didn't it rain this year? The water-givers in the sky must be angry. Virgin Sacrifice! NOW!"). I won't disagree that such primitive notions of God are irrelevant today, but as man has evolved, so has our understanding of God. I assert that as we continue to evolve, so does our concept of God. The final definition of God will not be reached, just as the full potential of humanity has yet to be realized. Our faith and belief in something beyond ourselves is not pointless.

Consider this: We have yet to find conclusive evidence that life exists in the universe other than on Earth, yet we believe it does as evidenced by our continual search of the cosmos. Why would we look if we didn't believe? Is it possible that we are alone in the universe? Yes. Is it likely? Probably not, and I don't think we want to entertain the notion that we might be. It is our faith, our quest for answers, and our desire to explore that keeps us moving forward.

4. **Karma is real**

Maybe not in the literal next-life-determined-by-this-life way, but in the what-I-put-out-comes-back way (which, upon further reflection, is the same concept, just on a different timeline). Whether it be through our thoughts, words, actions, emails, tweets, blogs, podcasts or voting practices, we are deciding what our immediate (and not-so-immediate) world looks like. In other words, we are creating our own reality.

When I'm really honest with myself, I have no choice but to admit that most of the hardships and difficulties I encountered were manifestations of negative thoughts, judgments and fears that I focused on earlier. Sometimes years earlier. Yes, there are freakishly random occurrences we seemingly have no connection to. We most likely don't. With so many people around us, there will be overlapping of experiences. It is how we deal with those experiences moving forward that will determine our future.

5. Our passion will support others

The 1952 Nobel Peace Prize recipient Albert Schweitzer has been credited with saying, "The purpose of human life is to serve and to show compassion and the will to help others." Living in our passion will support our own happiness, and it's not all about us. By being in service to others, we are spreading our sense of peace and compassion, and we become an example for others to emulate. My belief in living passion leading to peace comes from a life of not doing so for much of my youth. I discovered a love and talent for music at the age of 8, and my mother quickly enrolled me in classical lessons. I was not a prodigy by any stretch of the imagination, but I enjoyed playing. My music, however, was mostly an extracurricular activity, and by the time I reached my teens, I wanted to do what my friends were doing. There were problems, though: I wasn't athletic like my closest friends, I wasn't the brightest bulb in the academic box, and when it came to dating, well, let's just say I was a late bloomer.

While in high school, I chose my course of study based on my circle of friends, not on my field of joy. So instead of potentially fulfilling years of art and English and history, I suffered through the endless misery of chemistry and physics and biology. I should have gotten a clue when one year I failed every exam and had to repeat the entire year, but I stubbornly persisted.

Through it all, my suffering was tempered by my music. I discovered gospel and jazz. I experienced the miracles of playing by ear and composing. I joined the school orchestra and jazz band. I became a staple musician at my church and for other choirs. I added guitar and percussion to my repertoire of instruments. As a result, I expanded my circle of friends. My days became a routine of suffering through the school day to enjoy what came after. I eventually got the clue, so when it was time for college, I declared a major in music. But not just any music major—I chose music therapy. The funny thing was, I had not even heard of music therapy until I read a description in a college brochure, but when I read that paragraph, something in my soul screamed in recognition. It was no small feat convincing my parents to bankroll four years in a foreign country to pursue a degree that I could hardly describe.

Convince them I did, and I was off to Shenandoah University in the picturesque Shenandoah Valley of Virginia. Only thing was, I started college in January on the heels of a blizzard, and up to that point, I had never seen snow in my life. I was cold, lonely, miserable and depressed. No one had taken the time to give me a sneak peek of what to expect at college, and I was certain I had made a colossally gargantuan mistake. But I stubbornly persisted (a subtle yet recurring theme in my life), and with the exception of a few excruciatingly cold winters, I wouldn't trade my college experience for all the tea in China. I truly came into my own and went on to have a very successful music therapy career. My success was not only measured by financial gain but also by lives touched.

As a music therapist, I helped my clients and their families experience moments of joy and fulfillment. I worked with preschoolers to adults in daycare and with patients with various developmental and emotional disabilities. I worked in schools, rehab facilities, and then I ran my own private practice for a while. Although it wasn't always smooth sailing, being my own boss gave me a sense of satisfaction I did not know was possible. I was definitely living in my passion.

So why am I no longer a music therapist? It turned out that while I was living in one passion, another was silently brewing. While I was honing my music skills in church as an adolescent and teenager, I was also paying close attention to the minister. Initially I may have been caught up in the whirlwind of his powerful charisma, but I also remember intuiting, "I'm going to do that someday." It wasn't a deafening proclamation that consumed every moment of my day. It was more like low, soft whisper ... so soft I often didn't hear it or chose not to hear it because of the fears surrounding such a calling.

My crisis of faith in college would keep me out of church for a few years. When I found Unity, I also found a new view of God—a God with a tagline like a human resources disclaimer: "I do not discriminate on the basis of race, gender, ethnicity, religion, sexual orientation, or any other ridiculous reason you could invent as an excuse not to love someone else." Unity was a place I could explore my spirituality without fear of judgment or condemnation. And wouldn't you know, out of the blue, the whisper returned, but this time it was loud enough that I couldn't ignore it. But as I shared in Chapter 1, I tried my best.

When I decided to stop running, it wasn't the most glamorous shift into purpose. It came during one of my early morning journaling sessions in the midst of a stream-of-consciousness rant shortly after my return from the Lander mountain trip. Immediately after came peace. I didn't know what would come next or the logistics of the journey, but there was peace. My internal struggle was over. Of course, I couldn't quit my job the next day. I had a family to support (my wife was a full-time student), and there were steps to take before applying for ministerial school, but there was peace. It had been awhile since I had felt such a deep abiding peace; I don't know that I had ever felt it before. It was peace from a sense of knowing that this was who I am and what was mine to do that sustained me through the difficult periods of seminary.

11

You Got This!
→ The Question of Self-Doubt ←

OF 2 MINDS

"Blah, blah, blah! Blah? Blah, blah... blah!! Blah, blah."

I don't believe a word I'm saying!

@nakedpastor.com

"Doubt is the beginning, not the end, of wisdom."

This is one of my favorite quotes. It was penned by the semi-famous 19th-century author George Iles. I've often amended it to say, "Doubt is the beginning, not the end, of *faith*." For a quick example, look to the New Testament and the disciple Thomas.[21] His doubt led him to seek a more real experience with the resurrected Christ, and ultimately, a deeper unshakable faith. Isn't this ultimately what lies at the heart of all religions beyond the trappings and politics and dogma? An opportunity to experience a deeper unshakable faith?

I've learned that deeper faith comes about through simultaneously accepting and questioning. It's a paradoxical approach that is often met with resistance. Yet it results in a deeper understanding and more meaningful application of spiritual principles. I first accept the principle at a basic level of understanding. Then something may happen to make me question my understanding. I could either choose to remove it from my lexicon or refine it. Then comes a new acceptance, and the process repeats itself.

Take, for example, the idea of balance. I ... sorry, I mean Swami Ogunanda listed it earlier as a life lesson learned. One of the ways I live balance is by mostly eating healthy, and occasionally, I might wash down my double bacon cheeseburger and fries with a few beers. Or it's okay to be a couch potato today; I worked out yesterday.

It isn't quite the life-is-short-do-what-you-want approach; perhaps more like life-is-short-don't-be-anal-have-some-fun-but-don't-over-do-it. I began to question if this was indeed the best approach. The universe would answer in the form of a humble Buddhist monk.

The monk's name is Bhante Wimala,[22] without doubt one of the most amazing individuals I've ever met. *Bhante* means "venerable" — it's an honorific title. It's not his first name, even though we call him "Bhante." We crossed paths not too long ago at Unity Institute's Lyceum, and Jennifer invited him to visit our local Raleigh church, Unity Church of the Triangle. One of his requests was to bring "The Doctor." A practitioner of traditional Chinese medicine, "The Doctor" barely spoke English, yet diagnosed ailments with alarming accuracy simply by feeling the individual's pulse.

So there we were after the service, sitting on our front porch on a mild North Carolina fall evening—Jen, Bhante and me. Let me tell you, it was just a little surreal to be sitting on our porch on a mild North Carolina fall evening with a fully robed Buddhist monk, stuffing his face with baked kale chips. He sang "The Doctor's" praises as he recounted how she not only almost eradicated his lifelong allergies, but helped him avoid major surgery after an automobile accident. He admitted he was first a skeptic and didn't follow the treatments exactly as prescribed. This did not go over well with "The Doctor," who simply told him he could take her medicine or eat the things she told him not to, but not both, his choice. Jen said "The Doctor" told her not to drink alcohol. I jokingly, but on some level honestly, said maybe that's why I didn't go to see "The Doctor," because I didn't what to give up the occasional beer.

It was at this point Bhante lit into me ... sorry, got more animated and insistent. He said I cannot ignore my health any longer. He said now that he is having the best health of his life, he is also experiencing a deepening of his spiritual practice. He discovered that unless our physical form is at its peak health, we will be limited in how far we can go with our spirituality.

Bhante's admonishment made me question my perspective. Perhaps there are some things that should be out of balance. Can I really ever do too many of the things that make me healthier, stronger, more compassionate or more conscious? It might do me a world of good to totally give up the fried chicken and the bacon (whoa ... I actually just felt a pang of anxiety when I wrote "give up the bacon"). Can I really go wrong with exercising my body, mind and spirit every day? Sometimes it would seem too much of a good thing is a better thing. Plus, who would dare argue with a monk?

So I continue to question and embrace and internalize the spiritual principles by which I live to the point they are no longer an intellectual exercise but the very essence of my being. I call it Living in the Question.

Yet there is still a measure of faith I have yet to fully obtain: faith in myself. For as long as I can remember, I've been plagued by what has been termed the Fraud Complex: One day "they" will figure out that I don't really know what I'm doing and then it'll be all over. Now being the good Truth student that you are, you'd tell me to deny the power of such erroneous and irrational thinking and affirm otherwise. Which I have—and yet it still exists deep in me. I don't allow it to paralyze me as it did in years past, but it's still there, and in the process of accepting and letting go, I've made peace with it. Ever so often, when a new and exciting opportunity manifests, it raises its hackles and I hesitate. I blame it on my Gemini nature, or my Type 9 nature (if you're into the enneagram), and I wallow for a few minutes or hours or days; it varies. Then I snap out of it and move on. Ah ... the bittersweet nuances of my humanness.

Doubting myself has much deeper theological implications. Simply put, to doubt myself is to doubt God. Putting my faith in God is a concept I had apparently thrown out with my earlier understanding of God as an external and distant deity. If I now embrace God as the very operating principles of the Universe, the connecting space between us, the fabric of existence, and that I am the physical embodiment of all that, then how could there be room for doubt in myself? Wouldn't doubt in myself mean I truly don't believe, with every fiber of my being, in the truth of what I am, thus in God?

I could really wallow in despair on this. However, my salvation lies in my opening premise: Doubt is the beginning of faith. I am naturally imbued with, or have learned self-doubt, and as I mindfully explore and transcend it, I gain a deeper faith in myself, and in God. I can use the awareness of my perceived deficiencies as the fuel for my transformation.

Perhaps this is the hidden gift of my humanness.

12

We Should Repeal the Law of Attraction

→ The Question of Causality ←

WE SHOULD REPEAL THE LAW OF ATTRACTION

Like any good religion/sect/movement, Unity has a set of principles. We call them principles because, let's be honest, those of us recovering from more restrictive religions/sects/movements have too much baggage around the word *dogma*. Dogma has gotten a bad rap, but it's just another word for principles or tenets or beliefs. We have no shortage of those in Unity. If we have an issue, it's really around the sense of absolutism, finality, exclusivity, and personal suffering with which the tenets were shared and enforced. Unity co-founder Charles Fillmore encouraged folks to try on the principles and decide for themselves, not because he said so. While this is refreshingly liberating for a spiritual movement, it doesn't mean there can't be absolutism or the inflexible stance around a given interpretation.

Unity's teachings can be encapsulated in five basic principles[23] (each followed by my easy-to-remember contraction):

God is the source and creator of all. There is no other enduring power. God is good and present everywhere. (God Is)

We are spiritual beings, created in God's image. The spirit of God lives within each person; therefore, all people are inherently good. (I Am)

We create our life experiences through our way of thinking. (I Create It)

There is power in affirmative prayer, which we believe increases our awareness of God. (I Pray)

Knowledge of these spiritual principles is not enough. We must live them. (I Live It)

I'm on board with all these. I don't think I could be a Unity minister if I wasn't. And that's saying something, considering I thought they amounted to heresy when I first heard them. Growing up, I had been steeped in the belief that there was an evil entity leading the charge against God. It was like a comic book storyline playing itself out: The Devil (aka Lucifer or Satan) and his dark minions in a relentless campaign against God and the angelic forces of light; a war as vast as the cosmos and as enduring as time itself, yet with hourly skirmishes in my own consciousness. As a kid who loved comics, I resonated with this metaphor and was admittedly reluctant to give it up.

The truth is I liked having something other than myself responsible for my failings—the Devil made me do it; this was Satan's handiwork; I fell into a snare of the Tempter; I was deceived by the Great Deceiver. No, I'm not making those up, nor am I poking fun at the concept. Such views were a very real part of my thinking and personal philosophy. They continue to be for many, including some close family members, which always makes Barbados a bittersweet and potentially explosive powder keg of a vacation destination. Also true was the sense of relief and safety and reassurance I felt when I abandoned that line of thinking. I no longer spent my days feeling like I was manipulated or not in control of my own thoughts. I flicked that little red guy off my shoulder once and for all.

But here's the thing about duality: When you eradicate one half, it's not long before the other half has to go as well. No devil, no angel. When we say "there is only God," there really isn't a "there" as in location. It's a "there" of existence, beyond time and space—everywhere and nowhere and always and now. We often, and erroneously, think of God in finite terms because we are finite and linear thinkers. When we use words like "omnipotence" to describe God, we imagine a presence so vast it encompasses all that is. It's a step in the right direction, but I more subscribe to the idea that, as one of my favorite Unity authors, Eric Butterworth, put it, all of God is present at every point in the Universe. That means me too. And you. The entirety of the powerful-beyond-conceptualization creative principle of existence resides in and expresses as each and every one of the 7 billion individuals on the planet. It could explain the seeming chaos of our world today.

It's not all bad news though. The third principle is an invitation to consciously embrace and use our inherent creativity, which, unfortunately, can be a slippery slope if misinterpreted. It is the crux of prosperity teachings. We can have what we desire because we can use our creative power to bring anything into our lives. Treasure mapping is a popular example of this—stare at that picture of the car or house or beach you ripped out of a magazine and it will show up. The premise isn't entirely incorrect. I've used it myself. During the first prosperity class I took, I held the intention for a 1998 silver-gray Honda Prelude. Sure enough, on an unexpected detour while driving to work a few weeks later, I passed one sitting in a front yard for sale. I didn't buy the car. The moment I saw it, I thought, If I can make a car happen ... I succumbed to a metaphysical rookie's plight: greed. Realizing I had the creative power of the universe at my disposal, I overwhelmed myself with undefined flights of fancy.

I also made the tragic mistake of taking the principle much too literally. While nothing happens by accident or without a first cause, there is a line between intentional creation and the haphazardness of connectivity. Yes, I believe we are responsible for how our life shows up, but not necessarily those things that happen alongside it. For example, if I obsess over thoughts of lack, then that's all I'll see; nothing will ever be enough in my life, regardless of what I may actually have. I will always feel poor. I'll make decisions from that mind-set and might even create the poverty I had been trying to avoid. Or I might not—there are plenty of millionaires who still live with a consciousness of lack. But should a bolt of lightning strike my house in a thunderstorm and it burns to the ground, it wasn't because of my lack thoughts. Lightning happens.

Here's a can't-make-this-up-it-really-happened example of how the concept can be misinterpreted and misused. We all probably remember the 2010 earthquake that devastated the island nation of Haiti. Talk about kicking a people when they're down. My ire was stoked when I heard someone say that on some level it was the consciousness of the Haitian people that drew this experience to them because that's how the Universe works—anything that happens has an attracting consciousness behind it. Really?!? That's the same kind of crazy talk as Pat Robertson's ridiculous assertion that the earthquake was the result of an 18th-century pact with the Devil, or that Hurricane Katrina was God's punishment for Americans. What level of responsibility should we then place on the residents on Japan's eastern coast for the 2011 earthquake and tsunami?

There are so many ways to repudiate such illogic. For starters, if any geological or meteorological occurrence was the result of human consciousness, what was the cause before humans walked the earth? Why do hurricanes, floods and tornadoes affect people of all faiths? Why wouldn't it be summer all year round everywhere? The answer for all those questions is the same: We don't make it happen, neither does God. We never did, neither did God. There was a time when we thought God did, and that we could somehow convince God not to bring on the devastation, and if God did, it meant we did something wrong and deserved to be punished.

We're much smarter than that now, or so I thought. Some of us have changed our language and relocated God from a distant invisible realm in the sky to within our own consciousness, but we still have the same causation mentality: "What must I have done or been thinking to bring this disaster into my life?" Even worse, we try to be "helpful" by asking others what was in their consciousness. That is tantamount to spiritual abuse, or as I like to say, a bad case of "metaphysical malpractice."

If anything, because we are all connected to each other like strands in an intricate web of life, actions in my life will affect yours. But it doesn't stop there. It affects your life, then your friend's life because you're connected to them, then your friend's cousin's life, then your friend's cousin's husband's life. In this fashion, even though I don't know your friend's cousin's husband, I've affected his life in some way. He may not have attracted anything to him; he is simply connected to me and every other being on the planet. This idea has been popularized by the "Six Degrees of Separation" concept—everyone is on average six connections away from any other person. We also see it on a larger, seemingly more chaotic manner, with the "Butterfly Effect." It's most well-known theoretical example is the hurricane that started with the flapping of a butterfly's wings on the other side of the planet.

Jesus spoke to this in John Chapter 9 when his disciples brought a man who had been blind from birth and asked if it was his sin or his parents' sin that caused the disability. They were looking for a source of blame. Jesus said neither, that the man was born blind so that "God's works might be revealed in him." Jesus shifted the reasoning from causation to intention. Even as we live a life of conscious awareness, things will happen in our lives that we never saw coming—illness, death, natural disasters, accidents. Absolutely nothing in our consciousness drew this to us. What we have, however, is an opportunity: to apply spiritual principles and create a positively unexpected outcome; to show up for others, and ourselves, as compassion and forgiveness and grace and unconditional love; to be the hands and feet of benevolence.

We have it within us to create a global life experience of peace and abundance for everyone. It will only happen when we shift our thinking from "What's in it for me?" to "What can I put into it?"—when we no longer play the victim role by asking "How did this happen?" but choose to play the part of conscious co-creators by bringing and declaring God's presence as us.

13

Put Your Money Where Your Heart Is

→ The Question of Prosperity ←

Everyone remembers their first car. It was autonomy. It was escape. It was pride. It was status. It was responsibility. It was your trusty steed as you set out to conquer the world. It was where you feasted. It was where you slept. It was where you sang like no one was listening. It was where you cried like no one was watching. Your first car had as much meaning as your first kiss or the first time you had sex (both of which might have occurred in your first car) or your first apartment. It had more meaning if you paid for it yourself. It might have been a sparsely equipped compact that just rolled off the assembly line or a classic dream-come-true bucket of bolts.

Either way, it was a treasure, a symbol of some shift in life and livelihood, a modern day rite of passage, and you cried just a little on the inside when it was gone. Everyone remembers their first car. I've had a few first cars. There was the first car I was allowed to drive, the first car that was given to me, the first car I wrecked, the first car I bought.

Then there was the first car I didn't buy. Well, there were a lot of those, but this was a car that was proof of my ability to actually make something in mind come to manifestation simply by holding the intention for it. I was still fairly new to Unity, and taking a class called 4T: Tithing Your Time, Talents and Treasure for the Fullness of Life.[24] It was my first foray into the vast realm of prosperity consciousness, and I was skeptical. In 12 weeks I was supposed to be able to bring into my life whatever I wanted simply through the power of my thoughts? No wonder people think this is a cult! The premise was really about how to become an active and proactive creator of our own life experience, which doesn't sound so bizarre. But in the early weeks of class, it was an opportunity to see how far my beliefs could stretch.

The exercises were unorthodox, like repeating "I am prosperous" 100 times every day, twice a day, I seem to remember. We also had to come up with something we wanted to manifest in our life and share with the rest of the group. Everyone would state what that thing was, and for 12 weeks, or until that thing showed up, we would verbally support, affirm and hold the intention for each other.

Here's where the car I didn't buy comes into the picture. I was still driving the first car I had ever bought: a 1984 Toyota Celica GT, purchased with a touch of aggressive bargaining at a car auction when I was in college. At the time, she (yes, she) was great for short trips between my house and campus and, of course, the occasional mandatory college road trip.

She was not fit, however, for a daily commute on the Washington, D.C. Beltway, and problems kept mounting: electrical, mechanical, structural (I could see the road through rusted holes in the floorboard). The lack of air conditioning didn't help either. So I decided that it was time for a new car, but not just any new car. Using the principles I was learning, but not quite believing, I would manifest a 1997 fourth generation silver-gray Honda Prelude. It was my dream car at the time, and given the existence of Bentleys, Ferraris and Lamborghinis, I was obviously a small dreamer.

One morning, during the fourth week of class, I had to take a detour on my way to work because of a road repair in progress. As I meandered through a neighborhood, what do you think I saw parked on a front lawn with a "For Sale" sign wedged under the wipers? Hint: It wasn't a Bentley or a Ferrari or a Lamborghini. I stopped in front of the 1997 fourth generation silver-gray Honda Prelude, slack-jawed, eyes bulging, with the thought, Holy crap! This works! Repeating in my head like a stuck record.

The logical and reasonable ending to this story would have me marching up the walkway, ringing the doorbell, and making a purchase. But as I mentioned before, I didn't. Why not? After the initial shock, I became very afraid. For the first time, I began to believe in my innate Divine power, and I had a glimpse of the awesome responsibility that came with that power. I didn't think I was ready for it. I didn't think I deserved it. I didn't buy the car. I didn't tell the group about it either, at least not right away. I felt ashamed of my response. I mentally checked out for the rest of class, feeling like a failure. When I finally confessed to the rest of the group, a very wise person reminded me that manifesting a car in four weeks was nothing short of a miracle, and if I could make a car appear, what else was I going to invite in to create the life I wanted? Something clicked with that question. Yes, I could attract to me the things I needed to create the life I wanted! Although this was the point of the course, for some reason, I was really hearing it for the first time.

I was emboldened, empowered and, to be honest, a little cocky. As things began to show up with little effort on my part, people started calling me Mr. Manifester. I didn't stop them. Here's a good example: Jen and I had been talking about living together in her tiny apartment, which was really a converted two-car garage. It was nice, but barely big enough for one person, and it would've increased a long-enough commute by another 20 minutes. Plus it would have been me moving into her space. I thought we had a better chance of harmonious cohabitation if we started out in neutral territory. Jen wasn't happy with having to move, so she struck a bargain: "Fine. If you can find us a townhouse halfway between our jobs inside the Beltway for less than $1,200 a month, I'll move in with you. Good luck with that, by the way." My response? "You got yourself a deal. Start packing!" I never even had to look in the classifieds. Within three days of our agreement, a church acquaintance randomly said to me, "If you happen to know of anyone needing to rent a townhouse, let me know." She was a property manager with a vacant townhouse right inside the Beltway so perfectly situated that it would give us each about a 30-minute commute to work. Rent? $1,100. Bam! Just like that, I manifested our perfect first home. And later the second. And every house after that.

Something else was happening along the way as well. I soon noticed that I wasn't necessarily feeling any happier with the things I was bringing into my life. Unexpectedly, I was sinking into a sense of despondency that I was having trouble shaking. I was beginning to learn a lesson of the ages: Possessions do not provide happiness. The "Fullness of Life" described in the 4T program extended beyond the comforts that tangible things would provide. To be truly prosperous meant to be living a life in which, yes, physical and emotional needs were taken care of, but a deeper, more pronounced sense of fulfillment was achieved. *Prosperity* is more than a simple word. It can denote our economic welfare. It can be a reflection of our self-worth. It can be something we aspire to or something that causes resentment. It is difficult to define.

Case in point, there are more than two dozen Chinese characters that illustrate the various meanings of prosperity. We can think of prosperity in two broad categories: The "Seen" and the "Unseen." The "Seen" or visible prosperity in our lives is material prosperity.

Our possessions and even our relationships make up this part of our lives. We have witnessed the effects of trying to acquire too much material prosperity. It consumes us and we define ourselves by the pursuit of it. We become what we have. All our energy becomes focused on maintaining and amassing, and it becomes a source of stress in our lives. Unfortunately, we sometimes attempt to relieve that stress with more, not less. When we realize the futility of our efforts, we can become depressed. Dr. Andrew Weil, in his book *Spontaneous Happiness*, actually refers to depression as a "disease of affluence." The opposite is also true. We can define our material prosperity by what we don't have, labeling ourselves as "poor" or "failure" along the way.

There is the "Unseen" or invisible prosperity as well. This is spiritual prosperity. This kind of prosperity relieves, not adds, to the stress in our lives. Thomas Merton, a 20th-century Christian mystic, wrote that "anxiety is a mark of spiritual insecurity." When our consciousness is aligned with the true source of prosperity, we no longer live from a place of worry or concern. What is that source? It is God, the underlying and creative Principle of the Universe. It is in us, and we are in it. Unity co-founder Charles Fillmore defined prosperity as "the consciousness of God as the everywhere present resource." Can you imagine living from a knowing that God is the "abundance at the back of all things," and that there is no limit to our supply?

Supply of what, you might ask. I would suggest our supply of all that we need to live a truly prosperous life; to live what I call A Life Fulfilled—a life of abundance, greatness and plentitude. It is a life in which we live our heart's desires in ways that serve all humanity. It is a life where our needs are met effortlessly without fear or resistance. So what do we really need? Not what the fickle modern culture has told us we should want ... but what are each of us essentially hoping for or working toward every day?

If you take some time to think about it, you might come up with a list that includes the following: to love and be loved; to find and live my passion; to have my basic physical needs met, such as food, shelter and safety; to express my creativity; to have peace of mind; to have a healthy mind, body and spirit. Few material possessions are needed to meet such a list; certainly not billions of dollars. As you have seen in the news, many billionaires do not live A Life Fulfilled. For that matter, nor do many middle-class or lower-income individuals. A Life Fulfilled is a state of consciousness we bring to all that we do. Prosperity is part of our consciousness of being. We live from such a place through the power of Intention.

Intention is usually thought of as having a strong sense of purpose or determination. For example, we hold a thought or desire in our mind's eye and focus on it repeatedly. We can think of intention another way. It isn't something we do; rather, it's a consciousness that exists beyond us. In *The Power of Intention*, author Wayne Dyer writes that "Intention is infinite potential activating your physical and nonphysical appearance on Earth." In other words, just as we embrace a consciousness of God as the abundant, everywhere, present resource, we can align ourselves with omnipresence of Intention. We don't "do" intention, we embody it.

So I propose we step into something I call "The Prosperity Intention." It isn't something we do, but rather a consciousness from which we live: a consciousness of abundance, peace, prosperity, generosity, compassion, joy and so much more. How do we get there? By practicing the following five states of being until they become part of our authentic self:

1. UNSHAKABLE FAITH

When I use the term "Unshakable Faith," I am referring to Understanding Faith. This type of spiritual faith is beyond hope, blind faith or simple belief. While these are important stages of development, they are not the same. Understanding Faith is a deep abiding knowing that there are spiritual laws and principles that, when applied, will yield tangible results. It is a "knowing beyond knowing," for example, that this is an abundant Universe. It is engrained into every fiber of our being that as we live from a consciousness of God, all our needs will be met effortlessly. Because it does not come from our intellect, it is not something we think about; it is how we are.

2. DECLARING OUR CHRISTHOOD

In this stage, we declare the truth of *what* we are, not *who* we are. There is an important distinction. When we speak of who we are, we are referring to personality-driven characteristics and avocations. For example, "I am happy" or "I am a singer." When we declare the truth of what we are, we are referring to Divine qualities, such as Joy, Wisdom, Abundance, Creativity and Love. Who we are is temporary: I may be a singer today, but I might not be two years from now. What we are never changes: I am Creativity—because of my inherent Christ nature, I am, and will always be, imbued with the creative power of the Universe.

3. GIVING

To be in a consciousness of giving means first to realize that everything is energy: money, time, life, compassion, wisdom. When we give, we are sharing energy as represented by the particular object. Money, for example, can be considered as a form of energy that allows things to happen. Our thoughts and feelings about money are also transmitted when we give money, or anything else. When we give, we activate a Cycle of Fulfillment. We create an energy vacuum that the Universe has no choice but to rush in and fill. The familiar saying "You reap what you sow" is telling us that the energy we give, and more important, with which we give, will be replaced by the same kind. Unity co-founder Charles Fillmore invites us to live from "the knowledge that substance is omnipresent and that [we] cannot impoverish [ourselves] by giving, but rather will increase [our] supply." We can never give more than an abundant, everywhere-present resource. And we will only receive when we give.

4. FORGIVING

Forgiveness, like Intention, is most often seen as something we do. We can think of forgiveness as not only an action, but also a state of consciousness. In both cases, forgiveness is the process of pouring love into a situation or even the memory of it. Every time we have thoughts of pain, resentment, anger or betrayal toward something or someone, forgiveness is the act of replacing them with love. Such negative thoughts disrupt the Cycle of Fulfillment, like massive boulders falling into a river, essentially damming its flow. When we forgive, or give love for those negative thoughts, they break down bit by bit, until they may appear as harmless pebbles on a river bed. To forgive is not to forget, but it is to heal and restore the flow of consciousness in our lives. To live in the consciousness of forgiving is to constantly live in Divine Love, live from Divine Love, and to give Divine Love.

5. GRATITUDE

Unity co-founder Charles Fillmore calls gratitude the "great mind magnet." Giving thanks increases the flow of good in our lives. When performing miracles, Jesus would give thanks for the outcome before it came into being. Giving thanks allows us to see differently. It shifts our perspective so that we no longer focus on what is missing, but what has been there all along. Our consciousness shifts from one of lack to one of abundance and sufficiency. We realize the fullness of a life that is already present, and in doing so, we gain clarity of insight into what is really important in our lives.

I'll be the first to admit that it's difficult to take on a consciousness of prosperity when there are mounting bills to pay, when jobs have been lost, when homes have been repossessed. As I write this, it's been more than three years since I've had a full-time job. I've been ordained for almost a year, and I optimistically call myself underemployed. Yes, I'm fortunate enough that one of us in the household has a steady job, and I've come to a place of absolute certainty that no one can put a price tag on living a life of authentic expression. I turned down a job that would have prohibited me from doing the one thing I love as much as, if not more, than writing: speaking to a spiritual community on Sunday mornings. It was initially a difficult choice because it felt like I wasn't doing the "right" thing. Who would turn down a decent paying job in this economy with the bills we have to pay? But I knew if I did, I would find myself slowly dying on the inside because I wasn't doing the thing I loved. Speaking feeds me, sustains me, allows me to express my authentic self, and I am more fulfilled for it.

What fulfills you?

14

Better Me, Better Us
→ The Question of Relationships ←
as Spiritual Practice

HOW YOU DO ANYTHING...

...IS HOW YOU DO EVERYTHING.

Call me "Somebody" since it appears to be my nickname. When my wife would say, "Somebody needs to take out the trash" or "Somebody needs to vacuum the floor" or "Somebody needs to empty the dishwasher" or "Somebody needs to do a load of laundry," it's fairly obvious she's talking about me. One day I finally said, "Should I just get my name officially changed to 'Somebody'? It might be confusing because I was just getting used to the royal 'We.'"

I posted something to that effect on Facebook, and a friend sent me the following story. I had never heard it before but it quickly became one of my favorites for obvious reasons.

> There was an important job to be done and Everybody was asked to do it.
> Everybody was sure Somebody would do it.
> Anybody could have done it, but Nobody did it.
> Somebody got angry about that because it was Everybody's job.
> Everybody thought Anybody could do it, but Nobody realized that Everybody wouldn't do it.
> It ended up that Everybody blamed Somebody when actually Nobody asked Anybody.

Since then conversations at home have gone like this:

Jen: Somebody needs to take the recycling to the curb.

Me: Yes, but Anybody could do it, you know.
Joy: So does that make me Nobody? I don't want to be Nobody!

Relationships can be challenging. No wait ... relationships *are* challenging. Anyone who has been in one for more than six minutes can attest to that truth. We like to think it's the other person who makes the relationship challenging. You might think, If only they were more like me, this might go smoother, but that train of logic is steaming its way straight into the side of a mountain for a spectacular crash. If I were in relationship with someone exactly like me, I don't think we would have lasted 13 days, much less 13 years, which is how long I've been married to someone who is mostly, and thankfully, *nothing* like me. If I were in relationship with me, here are a few things that I'd have to tell me because they would drive me crazy:

- Shoes have a place and it's not the living room or the dining room or the kitchen or the family room or anywhere you happen to sit for more than two minutes.
- No matter how often you put dirty dishes in the sink and leave them to their own devices, they're not going to give themselves a bath.
- The clean laundry is not going to fold itself, and you have drawers for said clean laundry, so please stop living out of the laundry basket.
- Put the cordless phones back in their base. Yes, I know cordless means you can walk with them, but when they all end up in the same room with dead batteries, who's going to be making a call then?
- Speaking of cordless phones, when you get a call, please take the handset to another room. I shouldn't have to turn down the TV so you can have a quiet conversation.
- You're not 7 years old. Peanut butter and crackers is not dinner.

- There's really no need to go through four pairs of socks every day when you wear the same pair of jeans for four months without washing them.
- The grass needs to be cut when it reaches a certain length, not when you feel inspired to do it.
- The recycle container is just outside the kitchen door—creating a pile of items to recycle on the counter just inside the kitchen door seems like a half-hearted effort.
- Just admit that regardless of how many tools you own and the good intentions you have, you're not a handyman and things are worse after you "fix" them.
- When we go out to eat, don't order what you want and then eat my food.
- You can't always have the food your way; every restaurant is not Burger King.
- Everything I say is not worthy to be tweeted or posted on Facebook.
- When we agreed not to have a TV in the bedroom, it implied not watching your favorite episodes on your iPad.
- I know you're a one-sport guy, but I still exist during basketball season.
- I'm sorry it's 3 a.m. and you can't sleep, but there's no need for both of us to suffer.
- No, I wouldn't say you snore loudly; I enjoy sleeping by myself in the room farthest away with earplugs in and a pillow over my head.

Evidently I'm not the ideal person to live with, yet for the past 13 years someone has, and not against her will either. How has she been able to survive my "personality uniqueness" and me hers? Not by trying to change each other; we tried that for years and it didn't work. All it did was support the story we created about what was wrong with the other person that was preventing the relationship from being the best it could be. As that story became more reinforced, it drove a wedge of resentment deeper between us. In spite of that, we were committed, which was about all that kept us together through the worse times.

The times, for example, when my crises of faith and self caused me to doubt everything, including my love for the person who loved me the most. We were at least smart enough to know the times we needed help. We saw our fair share of couple's counselors, read our fair share of relationship books, did our fair share of bonding rituals. While these things helped us navigate through the uncharted waters, they never seemed to be long-lasting fixes. By this time, we'd been together almost 10 years and it felt like we still hadn't found our "groove" ... if such a thing really existed. I thought it should; did the work of relationship really have to be this hard?

Then something happened. Something we didn't plan to do but did anyway. Something, in hindsight, the counselors had hinted at but never said outright; something that initially seemed antithetical to relationship best practices. Something that I think we knew all along but never fully embraced. We stopped working on each other and worked on ourselves. We realized that we were the relationship, and if we wanted the relationship to be the best it could be, we would have to bring the best of ourselves to it. It dawned on us that we had been devoting much of our energy to learning how to be the best at what we do, and very little of it to discovering the best of who we are. I was so trying to be the best husband I could be, I was paying little attention to being the best "me" I could be, and I came before any role—spouse, parent, student, employee, son or brother. Let's be clear, while extremely important, these are just roles we play. They don't define who we are; they become what we bring to them. Perhaps then, the greatest work we could ever do for any of our relationships is to find and nurture the best of ourselves, then share that with those around us.

As it so happens, being in a relationship, especially a long-term one, is one of the greatest opportunities to discover the best of ourselves. Why? The idiosyncrasies of another become a flashlight, or in some cases a floodlight, that illuminate the shadowy corners of ourselves we would rather ignore and leave to gather dust and cobwebs of unawareness. Like anything else that increases self-awareness, relationship becomes a spiritual practice. When we take the time to observe our reactions and trace the thinking behind them to the root of our issues, we find the pieces of ourselves that require the healing touch of love and forgiveness. We discover wounds that have gone untreated for so long that the pain of them has found a permanent place in our psyche. We can begin, piece by piece, step by step, the journey to wholeness.

Many of us, however, don't allow ourselves the gift of this opportunity because we get stuck in the efforts to change the other's behavior. Any of the examples above illustrate this, and by way of true confession, my wife and I compiled that list together about each other. We had a good laugh while we were doing it, and no, I won't reveal which was whose—it wouldn't be appropriate. All right, you twisted my arm. I will give you one, but purely for academic reasons to properly illustrate my point:

I used to become angry when I could hear the phone ringing but couldn't quickly find any of the handsets to answer it. Jen was in the habit of leaving them in whichever room she last had a conversation. Sometimes by the end of the day and four conversations later, they would end up in the same room, buried under cushions or pillows.

Seriously—was it that strenuous a task to bring the phone back to the room it came from? We don't live in a mansion! (And if we did, we could afford to hire someone on staff just for that job. Ridiculous, I know.) I would make long-winded speeches about defeating the purpose of having a phone we couldn't answer, about batteries dying and not being able to make a call in an emergency, about being inconsiderate to others. I would make a big show of returning a handset to its base, leading by example, painting the picture of a simple yet heroic effort to be emulated by all. Look at me! Saving the world from the plague of misplaced gadgets!

Yes, I put that much energy and effort into the location of a cordless phone handset. At some point, even I could see that my reactions were excessive for the crime. But why was I being triggered like that? What wounded piece of me was being prodded to cry out? What healing and forgiveness needed to happen? The answers didn't reveal themselves for some time. They rarely do. Often the scars of trauma are buried deep beneath layers of protective habits, behaviors and personality traits we've plastered on to avoid feeling the pain, or in some cases, to literally survive. But while I stayed open to whatever would reveal itself, I did what didn't come naturally: I changed my behavior. Although not easy at first, I would simply replace the handsets without complaining. Well, first I didn't complain out loud, then soon the inner complaining ceased as well. Sometimes I'd even force myself to leave the phones just where I found them to prove to the irrational part of me that the Earth wouldn't teeter off its axis and fling itself into a black hole at the other end of the universe.

As the anger and resentment subsided, the real issue slowly revealed itself. The out-of-place phones were threatening my sense of order. But why was order so important to me? After all, I was from the Caribbean. The very essence of don't-worry-be-happy-go-with-the-flow-if-it-doesn't-get-done-today-do-it-tomorrow was imprinted on my DNA. Apparently that wasn't enough to overcome an early childhood of chaos. A few years after I was born, my parents opened their first business together. It was a small two-aisled neighborhood grocery store. A real mom-and-pop affair when compared to today's mega-size shopping centers. They worked tirelessly for six and a half days (and nights) a week, and until I was 8, I was shuttled between them, a great-aunt on my father's side, and my maternal grandmother. I might have been young, but I remember feeling like I had no single place to call home.

Although surrounded by loving family, I felt lonely and displaced. I also sometimes felt disoriented because, despite best intentions, plans would sometimes change. When I was 8, business was doing so well my mother did not have to work nearly as much, so I lived with my parents full-time. Just as I was getting used to that change, I switched schools. I transferred from Montessori bliss to parochial hell. It was evident that my first few formative years were not exactly calm and orderly. It also become clear that, almost 30 years later, I was still carrying the pain of those years—pain that would be triggered by something so trivial; pain that probably would not have been triggered if I was alone or with a partner just like me; pain that was now exposed and ready to be healed.

Such is the challenge and gift of relationship. So goes the work and rewards of self-awareness. Going deep to learn about oneself is a lifelong exploration. It's a spiritual practice unto itself. Since we're expressions of a Divine Idea, to know ourselves is to know God. Fortunately, there are many tools to aid us on our inner expedition. The enneagram, for example, has been invaluable in my self-discovery, and I'm not exaggerating when I say it just might have saved our marriage.[25]

More than a simple personality assessment, it is a spectrum of personality styles. It taught us how we viewed the world, and ultimately, each other. It gave tremendous insights into how we developed our behaviors. It revealed aspects of ourselves that we didn't know existed. It explained why I would retreat and shut down in the face of conflict rather than endeavor to stay connected. More important, it provided a path to balance and wholeness that allowed us to see our differences as gifts, not sources of contention. It helped us to develop a deeper appreciation for each other. It equipped us to love without conditions.

According to the enneagram, there are nine types or styles that exist within us to varying degrees, and we tend to live mainly from one. It's really more like nine paradigms through which we view the world. I am a type Nine, Jennifer is a type One. Type Nines want to make the world a more peaceful place. We have the ability to see all sides of a situation and find common ground. We dislike conflict, and in a misguided effort to keep the peace, we sometimes make our own desires less important than anyone else's. Type Ones want to make the world a better place. They have high standards of excellence, striving to make sure things are done with honesty and fairness. They can be impatient when others settle for mediocrity, and they tend to put more pressure on themselves to be good than anyone else. A match made in heaven if I ever saw one!

Before our exposure to the enneagram, we would see some of each other's traits negatively, using them as evidence to justify our own righteousness. It doesn't take an experienced relationship counselor to see this was a recipe for disaster. The enneagram taught me that, as an unhealthy Nine, my tendency to withdraw in the face of conflict was feeding my sense of dissatisfaction and driving a wedge between us. It showed me how to get in touch with my latent creative energy and inspire myself. It also empowered me to take a gentle stand for my authentic needs and not lose myself in Jen's desires. Working with the enneagram got me in touch with anger issues I had previously denied. I wasn't the explosive type and saw myself as the standard bearer of "go with the flow." What I was doing instead was squelching my anger because peacemakers don't create conflict, or so I erroneously believed. My anger would seep out though as I quietly seethed and sulked for days, becoming a passive-aggressive monster along the way. It was slowly eroding my enthusiasm for life, my self-confidence, my calm center and our relationship.

As our attention shifted to developing the healthier attributes of our Types, a profound shift began to happen in our relationship. I saw that Jen's wish for me was to be successful and embrace the grand vision of myself that she saw in me from the day we met. She was able to connect with my desire to fully embrace the present moment and see the good in whatever was before us. As we learned more about ourselves, we were able to share the better parts of ourselves with each other. Rather than just seeing ourselves as two individuals in a marriage, we were now partners on a team who supported the growth and discovery of each other. As we learned more about each other's style, we approached our disagreements much more compassionately. We truly understood why the other's perspective was important to them beyond needing to be right. We could see the genuine motivation behind the other's point of view and how we could bring our own style into the mutual desire to find middle ground.

I used to think we were from different planets when it came to being in relationship. It seemed like we just weren't speaking the same language. It was less about the speaking and more about the way each of us was listening. We've learned to become aware of when we're only listening and seeing and being from a single paradigm. We now have the tools (nine to be exact) to better place ourselves in each other's shoes. We are now equipped to know ourselves better, and when we're better individually, we're better together.

A better me makes a better us.

15

Bah, Humbug!

→ The Question of Spiritual Evolution ←

QUESTION?: WHERE WERE ALL THE IMPORTANT PEOPLE?

- ANIMAL
- FOREIGNERS
- STRAW
- NOBODIES
- ANIMALS
- Unclean
- manure

Maybe Ebenezer Scrooge was on to something. Is Christmas really worth all the fuss and the stress? This most festive of seasons begins with a day ominously titled "Black Friday." Well, maybe for you it began with the pilgrimage to some relative's house for Thanksgiving. Or maybe it began when the "Christmas Carols 24/7" radio station started pumping holiday songs over the airwaves in October. But for the most part, the general agreement in our commercially obsessed society is that the unofficial start of the holidays occurs in the wee hours of the morning the day after Thanksgiving, when department stores facilitate a riotous ritual of too-good-to-be-true bargains that turn otherwise civilized shoppers into a frenzied mob. One would think the tryptophanic effects of the day's likely turkey overconsumption would bring on a mellower milieu, but alas, not so much. And the time that stores throw open the floodgates has steadily crept backward from dawn hours to 4 a.m. to midnight, into Thanksgiving Day territory at 10 and 11 p.m. Scrooge might not have minded the commerce part so much, but the rest of it?

The start of Christmas in our household is marked less by a predetermined day than by a specific location. The attic. Any event that starts in a cold, cramped place devoid of light can't be all that good, right? But that's where I find myself one morning during the first two weeks of December. Somehow every year the plan from the previous year to keep the boxes and tubs of decorations within easy reach goes awry, and I have to salvage them from the depths of the darkest, most cobwebby corners of the attic. We aren't the kind of people who label things, so after I've wrestled the containers down the precarious attic stair-ladder, we begin the terribly inefficient process of unpacking it all. Before long, it looks like Christmas has regurgitated all over the living room. At this point we usually divide and conquer. I head outside with the lights.

Ah, the lights—bright, sparkly and the bane of my holiday existence. No matter how carefully I wrap them and check to make sure I only pack away working lights, I always find them knotted and partially working. I swear there must be attic gnomes who wait all year just for this moment; do I hear thin branches scraping the roof or the snickering of patient mischief-makers? Anywhere from 20 minutes to it-shouldn't-have-to-take-this-long of testing and detangling and replacing and rebreaking, I risk life and limb on a flimsy aluminum ladder planted on uneven ground to make the house visible from outer space.

Should you think I'm being overly dramatic about the "life and limb" qualifier, one year I fell off the ladder into a holly bush. Despite the frequent pairing with ivy in a certain carol, there was nothing to hold onto as I landed among leaves prickly enough to be felt through two layers of clothing. Naturally, in spite of all the aforementioned testing and replacing of bulbs, all the lights won't work after I hang them, and the process starts all over again.

By dusk I'm either satisfied or I've surrendered, and I go inside to find the house has come alive with things that shine, sparkle and sing. A few of them do all three. From the combination music box/Santa snow globe to the holiday themed cushions to the unique and numerous crèche-inspired curios to the raucously loud singing tree (whose nightmare-inducing face suddenly appears and scares when the performance starts), virtually every flat surface is covered with some reminder of the season, lest we forget. There are hanging things too. There are stockings for people and pets. And mistletoe — I don't mind the mistletoe. This past Christmas we had a scare when Jen couldn't find her traditional decorating uniform: a horridly corny sweatshirt featuring caroling cows singing Christmas MOOsic. We never did find it, and I'll swear in court I had nothing to do with its disappearance.

We always decorate the tree last and together. Point of order here: Although we buy the tree before anything else happens, it doesn't necessarily mark the true beginning of the festivities. Depending on our schedule, the tree might sit forlorn in its stand for days. But to give it its rightful due, buying the tree is an event unto itself. Every year we agonize over choosing the perfect tree, which takes forever to pick out since we all have varying standards of perfection. By the time we've finessed it into or on top of the car, lugged it into the house, and repeatedly adjusted its placement in the stand, I (and strangely no one else) am covered in sap and the tree looks nothing like it did in the lot when we bought it. I admit I love the fresh scent of a Douglas fir or Colorado blue spruce, but it's nothing I can't get out of a can or a candle.

Back to decorating the tree: The lights go on first with much of the same testing, detangling, replacing and rebreaking the outdoor lights went through. Then it's time for the ornaments. As a family ritual, we buy a new ornament every year. We usually end up getting a one-of-a-kind handmade original from a craft fair or artist gallery. Combined with Joy's early preschool through first-grade creations and sentimental pieces from Jen's childhood, our tree eventually looks like it got rained on by a consignment shop. We're usually good about taking care of the delicate ornaments, but every few years there's a casualty. Once, while enthusiastically tossing tinsel strands onto the tree, Joy knocked off an ornament. It shattered into a million pieces as it hit the hardwood floor. My ear drums shattered into a million pieces as both Joy and Jen screamed from their respective upper registers. It was a cheap ornament, but it was one of a set of the four characters from *The Wizard of Oz*. Bye-bye, Tin Man. The set commemorated our time living in the Kansas City area and doing church with a small but oh-so-loving community in Manhattan, Kansas. On the way to church, we would pass the tiny town of Wamego, home of The Oz Museum, which ranks right up there with the world's largest ball of twine and the world's largest eight-ball if you're into memorable American Heartland oddities.

So with the emotions and decibels of the women running high, I did the manly thing and beat a swift retreat to the front porch with the excuse of needing to set up the crèche. It might have been the overwhelming day or the scene inside, but one look at the nativity scene and I was in a foul mood. I forgot how, year after year, decade after decade, generation after generation, we perpetuate this idyllic manger tableau that is nothing short of a drastic misrepresentation. I witnessed my wife giving birth. Trust me, there's nothing idyllic about it.

They were in a stable—more likely a shallow cave—that was home to farm animals and all the fragrances that accompany them. Given the housekeeping the innkeeper had to maintain at his primary establishment, I have my doubts about the stable's hygiene.

Speaking of why the inn was full, there is no historical account of any census conducted by the Romans, and if there was, it would have only been for Roman citizens, which Mary and Joseph were not. But for argument's sake, let's say the census did occur and Joseph needed to be registered; he would not have had to go to his ancestral birthplace. The Romans were masters of efficiency—they would not have engineered that kind of chaos!

Don't get me started on the Wise Men, or as I like to call them, the Unquantifiable Interlopers. "Unquantifiable" because their numbers are never stated. Tradition has assigned one Magi per gift (Gold, Frankincense, Myrrh) but they could have been any number. I call them "Interlopers" because they found themselves inserted into a scene they had not attended. A cursory glance at the story in Matthew (Chapter 2) informs us that they came after Jesus was born and the family was now living in a house. The problem is we have two narratives about the birth of Jesus (one in Matthew, the other in Luke) that are more different than they are alike. The unfortunate mash-up resulted in the presence of the Wise Men at the manger, along with shepherds who would have never left their flock in the hills if they had ever intended to work again.

I'm obviously not the first person to notice the flaws in the story, a Virgin Birth being the least of them.[26] I'm surely not the last to point out the added financial and emotional stresses brought on by the ironically titled Season of Joy. Yet the rituals and celebrations continue year after year. We reprise the same carols, rehang the same decorations, and pack everything up only to do it all over again 11 months later. But as I sat and fumed that evening, I begrudgingly admitted that no, it was not the same year after year. I only had to look at my own family to see that as we shifted from dating to marriage, from two people to three, from toddler to tween, from unaware novices to spiritual practitioners, so did our intentions and priorities and understanding around the season.

Case in point, last year we did not decorate until two days before Christmas. It shocked the living daylights out of even us. It wasn't a premeditated act attempting to prove a point. Life intervened and our schedule became fluid—fell to pieces was more like it. We surprised ourselves by not worrying or panicking about it. I don't think we would've responded so calmly in previous years. Correction: I'm *positive* we wouldn't have responded so calmly. Not getting caught up in the prevailing furor or even our own shame around how it might look to others reflected a sense of inner tranquility and purpose that was ready to be expressed. We were being in the world, but not of it. We are often inclined to believe the labors of our spiritual work have not borne fruit because our life patterns were not instantaneously transformed. It took us 15 years of spiritual study to not feel stressed by our late start; to accept the things unfolding before us and resist the urge to alter them; to be at peace with where we were on our spiritual journey.

So I needed to make peace with the Christmas story. Like a prudent apprentice, I turned to the teachings of the masters. I remembered that, absurdity aside, the Christmas story is also a metaphor of our spiritual awakening. Take Mary and Joseph, representing the heart and the head, the compassion and the intellect that combine and allow us to love with wisdom. Mary is our willingness to look beyond our own doubts and serve a purpose higher than ourselves. Her first response upon hearing the angel's proclamation of her future was "How can this be? I am a virgin." We, too, can step beyond our fears of inexperience when answering the call to something higher. Joseph is that part of us that is strong enough to take a stand for love and justice in the face of conventional prejudice. He had the legal right to end Mary's life, but he chose compassion in the face of certain ridicule, contempt and harassment. Their trip to Bethlehem reminds us of the journey of bringing our dreams to life. It might be long and under less than ideal conditions. Imagine being pregnant and riding a donkey! Jen had trouble getting from the couch to the kitchen when she was eight months pregnant, much less a 70-mile journey that could have taken a week.

Just as the couple found themselves homeless at the end of their journey, we, too, sometimes find ourselves in unexpected, seemingly hopeless situations. Lack of support from friends and family can catch us off guard. So can the outright rejection of strangers that have no room for our ideas. But fortunately, that's not how the story ends. Like the stable with a manger of soft straw, there will always be a safe haven at our time of greatest need. It goes by many names, but most call it *grace*. It's not the random favor of a distant God, but the assured outcome that comes through living our divine nature. We cannot predict what our "saving grace" will look like, but it will be there.

Which leads me back to my interloping friends, the Magi. All joking aside, they were courageous enough to leave their homeland and trek across the desert in an effort to bring resolve to an astrological event. We, too, have a star to follow. It might be an intuitive nudge; it might be the passion that makes our heart sing; it might be the divine idea that awakens us at 4 a.m. to send adrenaline surging through our veins. To not follow that star is to break the divine order of creation. All inventors, artists, authors, scientists, faced a crucial moment of choice: to let their ideas fade into memory or to bring them to fruition. No matter how daunting the road before us might seem, we have all the inner resources needed to make the trip, and that's what the Magi represent in us.

There are no guarantees it will be easy. Giving birth almost never is. I witnessed my daughter's entry into this world. Almost 12 years later, I am still awed by the feats of endurance called pregnancy, labor and delivery. Jen was nauseous for the entire pregnancy. She was in labor for almost two days. After one particularly memorable contraction, she declared that, just for the record, she had officially won every argument we ever had and would ever have.

The most mystical moment of Joy's birth occurred not when I held her in my arms as she gasped her first breath, but on the way to the hospital. We passed a church marquee that would later leave us speechless, but for whatever reason, Jen was the only one who saw it en route. Perhaps the Gods of Storytelling desired to enhance the tale. When she told us what the marquee said, we claimed it must have been a labor-induced hallucination, if such things exist. She insisted I go take a picture. I objected. But remembering that she had already earned victory in all disputes, and unable to resist the lure of a juicy fable, I returned to the church. When I saw the sign, for a brief moment, I thought I was also hallucinating.

To grasp the full gravity of the moment, you need to know that three months earlier, Jen awakened from a dream and announced that she had met the spirit of our daughter and she was to be named Joy. I didn't put much stock in the dream. Ultrasound pictures never revealed our baby's gender the entire nine months. Rightly so, when the doctor announced it was a girl, Jen found the wherewithal to exclaim, "I told you so!" The church marquee alerted us to the reality so poignantly encapsulated by the Christmas story, the tale of Ebenezer Scrooge, and my daughter's first moments in this world: "Sometimes Joy needs pain to give it birth!"

16

Zombies Need Love Too

→ The Question of Authentic Connection ←

As a minister and speaker, I like to think there isn't a topic I can't give a talk about. This assumption was once most severely challenged from the least expected source: teenagers.

Unity is known for its spiritual development program for high school students called Youth of Unity (YOU). It was one of the earliest established programs in the Unity movement. I was invited to speak at the church my wife was serving as associate minister. I was initially puzzled by the invitation considering it was one of the few Sundays she could speak, and she really looked forward to those Sundays. She told me that she was happy to share her speaking opportunities with me.

By this time, I had finished my seminary classes and interviews. The only thing that stood between me and ordination was the official walk across the stage at the ordination and graduation ceremonies, so I was happy for an opportunity to show off my newly acquired skills. What I quickly found out was that I got this gig because both she and the senior minister, who was conveniently absent, were at a loss on how to give a talk that featured a short cinematic treasure created by the YOU teens.

I couldn't blame them for passing the buck. After I saw the video that the teens conceived, wrote the script for (and *script* is a term I'm using with great generosity), starred in, directed, filmed and edited (yes, to their credit, there was postproduction work), I immediately emailed the church's Youth and Family Director the following response: "Funny video. And great acting. I can see the work that went into it. Now help me out a little with the point they're trying to get across?"

The video went something like this: A young woman using an online dating site plans to meet her date for dinner. The young man's profile picture looked exactly like the actor John Krasinski (Jim on *The Office* for you TV-holics). When her date arrives, to her horror but strangely nonpanicking surprise, he is a zombie. Perhaps not courageous or smart enough to run, she quickly calls a friend who apparently specializes in zombie neutralizations. He rushes into the restaurant, splashes an antidote in the zombie's face and it returns him to human normality just one frame later. At that moment, their order of brains arrives at the table. Cue the credits. The assignment the teens so creatively addressed was to show how technology can be used to facilitate connection. But you got that from the description, didn't you? Of course you did. I think the true feat of creativity accomplished was getting a sermon out of that three-minute exposé.

Joking aside, the video highlighted many issues characteristic of the human condition. First is the universal need to be connected to others. According to the Center for Nonviolent Communication, it's a core need that ranks right up there with things like physical and mental well-being, honesty, meaning and autonomy, which might seem contrary to connection but is really a necessary component of it. With connection comes the potential for belonging, nurturing, intimacy, trust, support and understanding. We all crave these things. We will do most anything for these things. I remember the feeling of disconnection when I first emigrated from Barbados to the United States; almost everyone had difficulty understanding my speech even though I was speaking English. My accent was so thick that in order to be understood, I had to learn to speak American. Trust me ... there's a difference.

When we go without these basic needs for too long, we suffer on many levels. Even in correctional facilities, the worst of punishments is solitary confinement. It is in connection with, and in relation to, each other that we not only define ourselves, but we see the face of the Divine. Yet why is something so basic to our existence often so difficult to achieve? Perhaps our desire for connection is thwarted because we attempt to connect with and from our egos and personalities and not what lies beyond them. So often we do ourselves a great disservice because of what we allow to stand between us and another—we don't find their physical appearance appealing; they hold a different political view; they don't run in the same circles I do; they are not in the same economic stratum as me; they are of a different sexual orientation; they observe a different religion; they are a different race or ethnicity; they are from another country; they speak a different language or have an accent; they are older than me; they are younger than me; they collect my garbage; they drive a Bentley.

The reasons we find to stay disconnected from others are staggering. What I find even more appalling are those of us who belong to religions or movements or groups founded on principles of equality and connection, yet we only practice those principles with others within our group who look like us, sound like us, live like us, spend like us, raise their kids like us, even die like us. When we think of others from these paradigms, we miss the most important thing about them, which happens to be the most important thing about us as well: Spirit. What do I mean by Spirit? I'm talking about the unchangeable Divine nature of each of us that comes from, is connected with, and returns to the timeless Principle that is God.

When the Bible refers to humans being made in the image and likeness of God,[27] I believe this was what the writers were referring to. It is the place at which the physical expression of Divine Essence begins. It is the energy of God within us. When we greet each other with the Sanskrit expression "Namaste," we are acknowledging the Divine within each of us, literally saying "I bow to your form" or "the Divine in me honors the Divine in you."

Connecting from Spirit is authentic connection. It reminds us that underneath the zombie masks of acculturation, we all have the same core needs. We may have differing beliefs of how we should meet those needs, and aren't we glad life is a tapestry of variance? When we connect from Spirit, we realize that encountering a different belief is merely an opportunity to learn more about ourselves. We learn about the other person too, but being self-aware involves questioning our own beliefs when met with opposing ones. Questioning a belief does not make it wrong, but it does ask if that belief still serves. It may have been necessary at the time it was adopted, but does it still hold true now? Maybe it doesn't. Maybe it does. Maybe it needs to be amended or enhanced. If the Constitution of an entire country can be amended, why can't my beliefs? Because I don't want to be proven wrong? Worse things can happen, and have happened, than me being wrong. In fact, being wrong has led to some of the greatest insights and improvements in my life.

Authentic connection requires us to be something we try our best not to be: Vulnerable. The definition screams of something to avoid: "capable of being physically or emotionally wounded or hurt." Who would want to put themselves in a situation to be hurt? Yet the very definition implies that in order to be hurt, one would need to be unguarded, open, willing and receptive. To be vulnerable is to risk sharing the frightened parts of ourselves; the places that we hesitate to explore, much less share; the resentments we have refused to forgive; the anger that still smolders; the pain that we have buried. To leave these unexposed is to bring a slow death to ourselves as we are consumed from the inside. The only way we can rid ourselves of such parasites is to shine light, love and forgiveness into our darkest recesses. This is the gift of being vulnerable and authentic in our relationships, for we often bury our pain and resentments so deep that we imagine we have forgotten them until another reminds us that we are still carrying them.

For many years, in an effort to prod me to greatness, my mother would point out my mistakes and deficiencies. It seemed that there was never enough I could do for simple unconditional approval. This eroded my self-esteem to the point that in order to salvage the last fledgling shreds, I cut off contact with her. It was not an absolute dissolution. Our relationship became a barely civil, infrequent, short series of conversations in which I shared nothing of myself, for if I shared nothing, nothing would be censured. For years, I sought to punish her by starving the bonds of our connection, and it broke her heart. This gave me no satisfaction. In depriving her, I was depriving myself. In breaking her heart, I was breaking mine. Yet when I realized this, I stood my ground, lost, having come so far through the dark forest of anger and unforgiveness I did not know the way back.

There is a saying that the journey of a thousand miles must begin with a single step. The original Chinese saying also translates as "the journey of a thousand miles begins beneath one's feet." What was beneath my feet? The ground of my being, my true authentic Spirit, my Christhood, my Buddha nature, the One Presence and One Power, the Silence. On this I stood, slowly letting love and forgiveness and gratitude and compassion seep into me, eventually guiding my first step, then my second, then my third.

I am still walking out of that forest, but now the path is becoming more defined, the undergrowth offers less entanglement, shafts of sunlight are streaming through a gradually thinning canopy. I know now that I cannot rebuild a relationship that never was, but together we can create something new, something authentic, something better.

17

This Sucks!

→ The Question of Self-Acceptance ←

"So... before I give you your test results, can I just ask if you believe in the afterlife?"

THIS SUCKS!

Confession: I have a thing for vampires. I should say I *had* a thing for vampires since I'm not nearly as obsessed as I used to be. But truth be told, you won't need to twist my arm today to see a good vampire flick. It began in the late '80s with the movie *Lost Boys*. As a Caribbean teenager, I was fascinated by the scary-but-cool twist on these creatures of the night. No offense to any *24* fans, but I maintain it's still Kiefer Sutherland's best work. I watched that movie more than a few times, always in secret though—admiration of such gory demonic influences was frowned upon in my family.

Things intensified in the early '90s. Between movies like *Bram Stoker's Dracula, Buffy the Vampire Slayer, Interview With a Vampire* and *Vampire in Brooklyn*, there seemed to be no shortage of creativity concerning the undead. The early 2000s didn't disappoint either. Two of my favorite trilogies rolled out: *Blade* and *Underworld.* The first *Blade* movie actually came out in 1998, but I didn't see it for a few years. Wesley Snipes epitomized cursed-yet-cool in the *Blade* series, and despite a forgettable plot, *Underworld* had two good reasons to watch—Kate. Beckinsale. By this time, I had also devoured almost everything written by Anne Rice, the standard for vampire fiction as far as I'm concerned.

Around 2005 the allure started to fade. The first of the four *Twilight* young adult vampire novels was published that year. The series would become all the rage. While I found this twist on vampire lore intriguing (vampires walking in sunlight suppressing their need for human blood), there was just too much teen angst for my taste. By 2008, when the ridiculously popular HBO series *True Blood* premiered, I had lost almost all interest in the subject matter—I've actually never even seen a single episode of *True Blood*.

Why do vampires strike such a chord with us? I can understand how we relate to comic book heroes—they represent a wistful desire to escape the limited normalcy of the everyday; they brush against our savior complex. Who wouldn't want to possess superhuman abilities of flight or strength or control of elements? Who doesn't wish to protect and be adored by the masses? Even the heroes with secret identities appeal to us, conveying the idea that there is more to us than meets the eye. But why would many of us find these characteristically malevolent creatures appealing? By all accounts, no matter which variation you subscribe to, vampires do not possess souls, so they cannot truly be alive. They are forever ruled by their thirst for blood. And what of the afterlife? What does that mean for them if they have no soul?

I suspect it is the very nonhuman qualities of vampires that we find attractive because they reflect elements of freedom we yearn for. They usually have superhuman strength and speed, seemingly able to defy the limitations of physics. They do not require rest, so they are not hampered by exhaustion. Vampires are passionate, sexual and not limited by social norms. In most portrayals, they are beautiful and sophisticated, amassing much knowledge and wealth from a greatly extended lifespan. They do not age, so depending on when they become vampires, they are forever young. They are also notoriously difficult to eradicate—traditionally a wooden stake through the heart or decapitation followed by cremation, but who, other than Buffy, is going to get close enough to do either?

Although not strictly immortal, do vampires provide an escape from our mortality? How often might we wish for more hours in a day as we fall into bed exhausted? How many things do we regret not doing as we endure the mundane busyness of life? I miss my youthful vigor as I approach 40 and admit that pulling all-nighters is out of the question, and the college diet days are long over regardless of my appetite. As I pluck the gray hairs from my goatee and lament over not being carded at the brewpubs, I sometimes fantasize about not having aged past 24. And I'll admit it—nothing makes me feel older than a cute college coed calling me "sir."

On the topic of mortality, let me digress for a moment and say something about the afterlife. There are all sorts of fantastic theories about what will happen after our hearts pump the final ounce and the synapses that light up our brains go dim. Some of us hold on to the idea that the soul will continue to exist in any variety of states— the hellish imagery of Dante's *Inferno*; a 72-virgin orgiastic extravaganza; a seemingly never-ending cycle of rebirth into another body; a paradise of our own creation; dissolving into the mystical energy of the Universe; a return to the Oneness and Love that is God. Some say nothing happens—no consciousness, no anything, nada. Despite the blissful anecdotes of light and love from those who have had near-death experiences, the truth is we don't know what will happen when we die. Was it fear of death that led to the creation of such stories? Is it the carrot at the end of the stick to manipulate otherwise clear-thinking men and women? Perhaps a tool to encourage righteous living in this life? Is it the fervent hope that there is more to our existence than this world because it would be just too depressing if this was it? I think we have more than enough to pay attention to in this life. The next will take care of itself. What really matters is how we live now, regardless of future reward. Okay, digression complete.

Vampires, fictitiousness notwithstanding, are the greener grass when we contemplate the downsides of being human. It is the human condition to want what we don't have. It's a condition dating back to antiquity—a condition serious enough to make the Top 10 list for moral living: "Thou shalt not covet ... anything that is thy neighbor's." The same applies to coveting parts of ourselves that no longer exist, or never did. Our society demands that we be in a constant state of want. Much of our economy is built around the desire for more and different. We are bombarded by messages that who we are is not good enough, pretty enough, smart enough, skinny enough or rich enough. We are taught to look down on others who are less than enough, and to be ashamed of ourselves when we think we are also less.

Vampires are also the embodiment of our shadow selves. Those are the parts of us that we dislike and have so suppressed that it would be painful to expose them to the light of day. For example, no matter my accomplishments, because of criticism when I was a young child, I began to believe I could never be truly successful. As I became an adult, I stopped subscribing to that idea, but to play it safe, I became withdrawn and shared less of myself. The practice became so ingrained that to this day, even after a fair amount of healing and therapy, I'm still reluctant to spontaneously share good news or successes; I relate to the isolation experience associated with vampires.

It's no way to live though. As much as I might have admired the glamorous representations of the vampire life, I don't want to ever be one. Not that I could since they're not real, but you get my drift. I don't want to be someone under the control of a thirst that will never be satiated. To continually yearn for what I don't have means I am dissatisfied with life as is. The key is to ask ourselves what that thing we wish we had really represents for us. Chances are we already are and have the very thing we are wishing for.

We think we want to be glamorous and ageless, but is it because we have not seen our own beauty at every stage of life? Superhuman strength? How about the strength of character it takes to be the voice for radical change or equality or the disenfranchised? Want passion? Try the heart-opening devotion and surrender of co-creating with a life partner.

Is it wrong to desire something else? Not necessarily—we might sometimes find ourselves in less-than-ideal circumstances. We have to remember, however, that they do not define us; we can change them. This is the beauty of spiritual principle. We are not doomed to an existence of perpetual craving. We are truly limitless in what we can imagine and bring about for our lives.

18

The Church Is Dead! Long Live the Church!
→ The Question of God in the Future ←

THE CHURCH IS DEAD! LONG LIVE THE CHURCH!

I have to start with a disclaimer: I'm going way, way off the beaten path in this chapter. I'm letting my inner geek out to romp for a few pages. While I'm at it, I might as well warn you: This chapter might be upsetting. You might be tempted to say, "He's finally done gone and lost it." Or, "How can this guy call himself a minister? Does he even believe in God?" You might even think I undermine the very spiritual perspectives shared in earlier chapters. This is why I buried the chapter here, at the back of the book. If it was an opening chapter, you might not have gotten this far. So as you read, remember that it's the "what if" in me taking a turn. I'm red-lining my power of imagination as I share my thoughts around the single premise that almost prevented me from becoming a minister: God is going to die. Yes, I realize the irony of someone in my profession making such a statement, so it goes without saying that an explanation is in order.

While I consider myself a "here and now" type, I spend a fair amount of time speculating about the future. Not just my future, but mostly about humanity's. Some of it is related to the choices I make today. As the Iroquois Law so eloquently stated, "In every deliberation, we must consider the impact for seven generations." Some of it, however, is pure technological fantasy. I am a geek at heart, if not in occupation. My occupation is fueled by the truth that, in spite of all our technological advancements, there continues to be more to us than meets the augmented-reality eye. We are spiritual beings. We have created spiritual community to nurture and remind us of our relationship with the Divine that exists in and around us.

As our understanding of the Universe (both outer and inner) expanded, our ideas around God had to evolve so God could continue to fit into our story of existence. We no longer hold the anthropomorphic view of God—a cantankerous, judgmental deity sitting on a throne in the clouds somewhere. Now God is within us, a spirit of Love, an energy of connection, a force of creation. We are also in God, a sliver of self-identified consciousness swimming in the sea of infinitum. Some of us push the limits and call ourselves God, assuming the creative responsibilities of existence itself. The question then arises: Do we exist because of God, or does God exist because of us? It's perhaps the ultimate Chicken-Egg question to which, ever the pragmatist, I answer "Yes!" The other question I ponder is this: Will there come a time when God no longer fits into our story? I know, I know ... Sacrilege! Heresy! But to be a good Truth student is to question the truth. As 19th-century author George Iles wrote, "Doubt is the beginning, not the end, of wisdom." So let the doubts begin.

Our understanding of this Divine relationship and the entities in it, ourselves and God, is both a product of belief and biology. Belief is required as we seek to establish a context of faith based on something that cannot be proved or disproved. Belief, understanding and even perception are products of our biology, more precisely, our brain. This soft, convoluted mass of gray and white matter is the hive of synapses and electric impulses that serves as the center of thought, feeling, intellect and our relationship with everything. It is the seat of our consciousness. Are we more than our brain? Some would say yes, and others would argue that everything happens in our mind, which I'll define as the product and process of the thinking, feeling, perceiving and interpreting that goes on in the brain. Then to add another layer of complexity, are we not of two minds? One that does the mental work and the other that observes itself doing the mental work? Indeed, the ability to know we are thinking and observe our own thoughts as though they were happening apart from us is what sets us above the other mammals; "Cogito ergo sum" (I think, therefore I am)[28] and all that.

So what does our brain have to do with the deific demise? It comes down to a hypothesized future event: the Singularity. It is the point in our not-too-distant future when, because of its exponential rate of increase, computing technology will surpass that of human brain computing power. It will be the dawn of true Artificial Intelligence (AI) capable of human-level cognition. We're not just talking about fast processing; there are supercomputers around today that can already process information faster than a human brain. The average brain is capable of 100 trillion operations per second (that's 100,000,000,000,000!). As of this writing, the world's fastest supercomputer (Japan's "K" computer) was clocked at 10 petaflops (or 10 quadrillion operations per second). That's 10,000,000,000,000,000![29]

Obviously speed isn't everything. There are certain ineffable characteristics of human consciousness that have yet to be replicated; otherwise, AI would be present reality. What makes the brain special isn't that it CAN execute 100 trillion operations per second, but HOW it does it, and the resulting outcomes. We don't just see colors, we create art; we don't just do kind deeds, we feel compassion for others; we seamlessly blend objectivity and subjectivity to create elements of life beyond ourselves. Can these distinctly human qualities be parsed and replicated? Some futurists believe they can.

Ray Kurzweil, perhaps the most outspoken of them, speculates it will happen as soon as 2045.

Before we collectively dismiss this as lunacy, you should know that Ray's been right about a lot of things. In his 1990 publication, *The Age of Intelligent Machines*[30] (while Microsoft was introducing the world to Windows 3.0 and Apple was shipping the Macintosh Classic), he predicted speech-to-text machines, real-time translating phones, conversing intelligent answering machines, and self-driving cars for the early 2000s. These predictions are virtually present-day realities. Amazingly accurate speech-to-text functions exist in almost every smartphone. When combined with instant messaging, translation applications, such as Ortsbo, MyLanguage, or Transfire, real-time conversation between speakers of different languages is possible. Most major companies have automated answering services that facilitate the narrowing of requests before speaking to another human being, if at all. Thanks to Google, self-driving cars are on our streets, although not yet at the point of mass production.

In 1999 Kurzweil made predictions for the following 10 years in *The Age of Spiritual Machines*.[31] These included personal computers with high-resolution displays ranging in sizes small enough to be embedded in clothing to the dimensions of a thin book (iPad), wireless communication between devices (Wi-Fi, Bluetooth), and personal computers for $1,000 performing a trillion calculations per second (in 2006 graphics card maker Nvidia introduced graphic processors capable of 3 trillion calculations per second). In his latest book, *The Singularity Is Near*,[32] he speaks of reverse engineering the brain by the mid-2020s, and nanobot technology being commonplace by 2030. We may be well on our way.

In 2005 scientists from Rice University developed a molecule-sized "nanocar," complete with chassis and carbon molecules for wheels.[33] In a 2012 study, scientists from Rice University and the University of Texas MD Anderson Cancer Center reported enhanced effectiveness and reduced toxicity of an existing treatment for head and neck cancer in mice using nanoparticles to deliver the drugs.[34]

So assuming Kurzweil and other futurists are right about the Singularity, the looming question is what happens next. The truth is, we can't predict what will happen next. Even Kurzweil acknowledges it will be such a game-changing event that our evolutionary path will be altered in ways we can't fathom now. But that doesn't mean we can't have fun guessing. There are way too many rabbit holes we could go down with this; the philosophical and ethical implications are staggering. Being the minister that I am, I'll keep it in a theological context while I don my futurist cap.

Earlier I stated that the brain was the seat of our consciousness. Some of us spiritualists might not want to entertain such a notion, and to be perfectly honest, I am willing to admit I could be wrong about this. But when I read of Dr. Jill Bolte Taylor's experience, I have to wonder.[35] Taylor is a Harvard-trained neuroanatomist—a brain scientist. In 1996 she experienced a severe hemorrhage in the left hemisphere of her brain. Being the scientist she was, she was able to objectively observe everything that was happening to her as her mind deteriorated to the point where she could not walk, talk, read, write or recall much of her life. Without the left side of her brain functioning, the side that controls language, categorizing, analyzing, describing and judging, her consciousness shifted fully into present moment thinking. She reported feeling "at one with the universe." Is that what "Oneness" really means and feels like? The neurological suppression of the practical and meaning-making side of us?[36] (After eight years of brain-building exercises, Dr. Taylor returned to full mental functioning and, among other things, penned her best-selling memoir *My Stroke of Insight*.)

My goal here is not to belittle the authenticity of spiritual experience. There was a time we believed the weather was the work of the gods. Knowing the science behind weather does not take away from the importance of rain in the cycle of life. In fact, thanks to science, we can now seed clouds and, in essence, control elements of the weather. Likewise, with the onset of the Singularity, there might be enough computing ability to finally understand the deep workings of the human brain. We might be able to grasp the mechanics behind thoughts, emotions and beliefs. Technology might allow us to measure and map the brain's every electrical impulse. Every feeling, memory, personality nuance, developmental quirk or (brace yourself!) spiritual belief could be identified and, because they are essentially electrical impulses, possibly replicated. In other words, there may come a time when we can quantify and copy consciousness.

Should that time come, will we still need God? And by God, I mean the nomenclature we have placed on currently unexplainable phenomena such as spiritual energy, or the awareness of an expansiveness beyond ourselves, or faith itself? As someone for whom some form of the Presence of God has been as real as the air I breathe, the thought more than unnerves me. Yet I do myself no favors by not exploring it and making peace with it, so that I may be of support to others should such a time arise.

If the supercomputers of tomorrow allow us to scan our consciousness, then we can consider some I-say-interesting-you-might-say-insane possibilities. I could load it into a very human-looking android. Will it still be "me"? If it is me, then could I be in two places at once? I could send my consciousness to any waiting android electronically anywhere in the world, not quite beam-me-up, but fairly close. I might then reload the experiences of android me into human me, and they become a new additional reality. Would I be able to tell the difference between what human me and android me experienced? Will the brain be able to handle the shift from linear time to simultaneous self-occurrences?

Here's the most worrisome element: If we can scan our consciousness into mechanical form, death truly becomes a choice. To remove the certainty of death is to redefine who we are as humans. For better and for worse, knowing that we have a finite amount of time to live influences our choices. It is the very impermanence of life that drives us to give it meaning and purpose. Whether we are aware of it or not, death defines us. It also plays a major role in our spiritual views. At one time, immortality was reserved for the gods. Even in our evolved thinking, we define God as infinite ... beyond space and time. What will we think of ourselves and God when we eliminate the limitation of time? As technology's exponentially increasing power continues to break barriers, will we lose God along the way?

An obvious possibility is that, as we transfer our consciousness from one form to another, God comes with us; as we evolve, God evolves along with us, or at the very least religion will. On the issue of God in the future, Kurzweil writes:

> Evolution moves toward greater complexity, greater elegance, greater knowledge, greater intelligence, greater beauty, greater creativity, and greater levels of subtle attributes, such as love. In every monotheistic tradition God is likewise described as all of these qualities, only without any limitation: infinite knowledge, infinite intelligence, infinite beauty, infinite creativity, infinite love, and so on. Of course, even the accelerating growth of evolution never achieves an infinite level, but as it explodes exponentially, it certainly

moves rapidly in that direction. So evolution moves inexorably toward this conception of God, although never quite reaching this ideal. We can regard, therefore, the freeing of our thinking from severe limitations of its biological form to be an essential spiritual undertaking.[37]

In *Rapture for the Geeks*,[38] author Richard Dooling reminds us that if history is any guide, the belief in God will persist: "If the Black Death and the concentration camps didn't stint humankind's God instinct, a race of ruling supercomputers probably won't touch it either." He predicts the development of new post-Singularity religions with new prayers, sacred texts and saints, such as Linus Torvalds, the inventor of the open source Linux operating system. He envisions computer historians revising notable religious texts to fit into the new era.[39]

Yet I believe that should we become something almost unrecognizable to our current selves, more mechanical than biological, our focus will shift from asking about our spiritual nature to preserving our human nature. There is no question that we will become more dependent upon technology, perhaps too dependent. As it literally becomes more of who and what we are, generation after generation will remember less about what it means to be human. That is unless we consciously seek to preserve its meaning.

I believe this is what "church" will become in the unforeseeable future: a remembrance and celebration of what it means to be human. It will be an occasion to honor that time in our history when we were more than electrical impulses reduced to the best logical outcomes. At our best, we were pillars of strength, creators of wonder, angels of compassion. At our worst, we were mongers of fear, harbingers of doom, proponents of violence. We always had a choice.

If I have any fears about the post-Singularity world, it is that we will increasingly turn our decision-making over to the supercomputers and trust ourselves less to make the mistakes that have helped define us and teach us about ourselves. Choice (aka free will) is the gift that allows us to manage, overcome and surpass our base instincts. If the mysteries of the Universe gave us God, choice gave us the ability to relate to God, or spirituality.

This prognosis for the future fueled my crisis of faith for a while. Then I remembered "when" I was: in the present. In this moment, my consciousness, as much as I can and can't explain it, is the first cause of my existence. Through trial and error (lots of error, by the way), I know that living from a place of spiritual consciousness and awareness creates a life I want to wake up for every day. I think this will be our saving grace as we forge ahead into the technological unknown. Even as we discover the how's and why's of our inner-verse, it won't take away from the feelings of wonder as we watch the setting sun, which we know isn't really "setting." To maintain the mystery in the face of fact gives depth and breadth to our lives. So while the geek in me excitedly awaits the final frontiers of technology, the Spirit in me rejoices in the beauty and majesty of life as we know it today.

OUTRO

So … about all that time it took you to read this book? I'm sorry to say but you're not getting that back. If it's any consolation, it took me a lot longer to write this than it took for you to read it. But I do want to thank you for reading it. I'm pleasantly surprised and genuinely grateful that you would honor me with your time and money (I'm assuming you bought this copy?).

By now, you must have realized I'm not your run-of-the-mill minister, which is saying something, especially in Unity. It's been a little more than a year since my ordination. In many ways, it feels like all I've done is back the car out of the garage without knocking over the mailbox and the garbage cans. Now I'm sitting behind the wheel, engine revving, slowly letting out the clutch (Of course, I drive a stick!), inching forward into the unknown. I don't know where the road will take me or how long a journey it might be or what adventures I will encounter along the way. Normally this would excite me to no end. But being a minister is no normal undertaking. It is often said, if you can do anything besides ministry, do it! Ministry isn't just an occupation or an avocation. It's both and then some. It's a commitment and a surrender. It requires leadership, but more often "followship." Ultimately nothing can prepare me for the fullness of it, and the only thing that will keep me at the ready is my own spiritual unfoldment.

Fortunately, I have a model of ministry to follow—a model that transformed the world two millennia ago. Jesus transcended and upended his world order by ministering to the needs of everyone, especially the outcasts and disenfranchised. He reminded us that our spiritual practices are not the goal, but the means to transform ourselves, and are ultimately useless if we treat each other without compassion. He allowed his divine nature to inform his humanity, thus becoming the idealized individual expression of that which we call God. He was the son of a carpenter from a flyspeck of a town in the Middle East, and we're still talking about him.

But make no mistake; he was fully human, just like the rest of us. So we have no excuse. I have no excuse to be any less of a transformative minister than he was. I simply need to remember the intention to serve. Serving others (and myself) from and through my heart is the fuel, the map and the vehicle for my journey of ministry. When I received my ordination, I accepted a commission to serve.

Former Girl Scouts' CEO Frances Hesselbein said it best: "To serve is to live."

This is my credo.

Again, thank you for reading.

And keep questioning.

Namaste.

ENDNOTES

Cartoons by David Hayward, aka The Naked Pastor, at *www.nakedpastor.com*.

All Bible references and quotations from the New Oxford Annotated Bible — New Revised Standard Version.

Chapter 1

[1] In 1976 Al Green was ordained, becoming the hippest minister I can think of.

[2] Green, Al. "Let's Stay Together." *Let's Stay Together*. By Al Green. 1972.

Chapter 2

[3] Jonah Chapters 1-2

[4] Music therapy is an established health profession in which music is used within a therapeutic relationship to address physical, emotional, cognitive and social needs of individuals. After assessing the strengths and needs of each client, the qualified music therapist provides the indicated treatment, including creating, singing, moving to, and/or listening to music. Through musical involvement in the therapeutic context, clients' abilities are strengthened and transferred to other areas of their lives. (Definition courtesy of the American Music Therapy Association at *www.musictherapy.org*.)

[5] Janice Millington (1948–2005) was a virtuoso pianist, violinist, composer and arguably one of Barbados' most influential music teachers. She taught music at the island's premier secondary education institution, Harrison College, for more than 30 years (I attended 1985–1993). A free spirit who would heap verbal abuse on her

students, her influence on some of the island's and Caribbean's pre-eminent musicians and artists cannot be understated. What started as a relationship based on fear and intimidation evolved into one of mutual respect. One of my life's highlights was introducing her to my family when we visited Barbados in 2003. Over tea, she pulled out a video of an award-winning performance I did when I was 15 years old that she had kept. Her tribute page can be found online at *http://www.myspace.com/janicemillingtontributepage*.

[6] Wile E. Coyote is a copyrighted cartoon character created by Chuck Jones in 1948 for Warner Bros. In the *Looney Tunes* cartoons, Wile E. Coyote concocts elaborate plans with absurdly complex contraptions in notorious failed attempts to capture his sole quarry, the Road Runner.

Chapter 3

[7] Durston, Kirk. "Just how many people *has* religion killed?" *www.newscholars.com*. http://www.newscholars.com/papers/Killing,%20Christianity,%20and%20Atheism.pdf. (Accessed May 15, 2012).

Chapter 4

[8] Loving v. Virginia (1967) was the landmark civil rights case in which the United States Supreme Court, in a unanimous decision, declared Virginia's anti-miscegenation statute, the "Racial Integrity Act of 1924," unconstitutional, thereby overturning Pace v. Alabama (1883) and ending all race-based legal restrictions on marriage in the United States. I was born in 1974, Jennifer in 1972.

[9] Luke 10:25-37

Chapter 5

[10] Cymbalta is a registered trademark of Lilly USA, LLC.

[11] *Friends* is an American sitcom created by David Crane and Marta Kauffman, which aired on NBC from September 22, 1994, to May

6, 2004. The series was produced by Bright/Kauffman/Crane Productions, in association with Warner Bros. Television. The original executive producers were Crane, Kauffman and Kevin Bright, with numerous others being promoted in later seasons. After 10 seasons on the network, the series finale (the 236th episode) was watched by 51.1 million American viewers, making it the fourth most-watched series finale in television history and the most watched episode of the decade.

Chapter 6

[12] A theory that financial benefits given to big business will in turn pass down to smaller businesses and consumers. *http://www.merriam-webster.com/dictionary/trickle-down%20theory*.

[13] Banks, Adelle M. "Church attendance down, congregations getting older, report says." 30 September 2011. *www.washingtonpost.com*. (Accessed May 15, 2012).

Chapter 8

[14] Kübler-Ross, Elisabeth. On *Death and Dying*. New York: Scribner, 1969.

[15] Exodus 13-40, Leviticus, Numbers, Deuteronomy

[16] Matthew 4:1-11, Mark 1:12-13, Luke 4:1-13

Chapter 9

[17] Rothberg, Donald. *The Engaged Spiritual Life: A Buddhist Approach to Transforming Ourselves and the World*. Boston: Beacon Press, 2006.

[18] Brown, Brené. *The Gifts of Imperfection: Let Go of Who You Think You're Supposed to Be and Embrace Who You Are*. Center City: Hazelden, 2012.

[19] Brown, Brené. *I Thought It Was Just Me (But It Isn't): Telling the Truth About Perfectionism, Inadequacy, and Power.* New York: Gotham Books, 2007.

Chapter 10

[20] Reportedly said by Einstein to a reporter who asked what the most important question facing humanity is. Actual source unknown.

Chapter 11

[21] John 20:24-29

[22] Find out more about Bhante's work at *www.bhantewimala.com*.

Chapter 12

[23] *www.unity.org/about-us/our-philosophy*

Chapter 13

[24] Created in 1988 by Rev. Stretton Smith. *http://4tprosperity.com*.

Chapter 14

[25] There are many online resources for information about the enneagram. I recommend *www.wepss.com* and *www.enneagraminstitute.com*.

Chapter 15

[26] Most modern theologians and biblical scholars have rejected the Virgin Birth storyline that is a common feature of many religions. For more on this, visit *http://www.entheology.org/pocm/pagan_origins_virgin_birth.html* and *http://hope-of-israel.org.nz/origins VBmyth.html*.

Chapter 16

[27] Genesis 1:26

Chapter 18

[28] Dictum coined in 1637 by French mathematician, scientist and philosopher René Descartes.

[29] Top500. "Japan's K Computer tops 10 petaflop/s to stay atop TOP500 list." 14 11 2011. *Top 500 Supercomputer Sites.* 7 4 2012. http://www.top500.org/lists/2011/11/press-release.

[30] Kurzweil, Ray. *The Age of Intelligent Machines.* Cambridge: MIT Press, 1990.

[31] —. *The Age of Spiritual Machines: When Computers Exceed Human Intelligence.* New York: Viking Penguin, 1999.

[32] —. *The Singularity Is Near: When Humans Transcend Biology.* New York: Viking Penguin, 2005.

[33] Rice University. "Rice scientists build world's first single-molecule car." 20 October 2005. *Rice University News and Media.* 7 April 2010. http://news.rice.edu/2005/10/20/rice-scientists-build-worlds-first-single-molecule-car/.

[34] —. "Nanoparticles may enhance cancer therapy." 15 February 2012. *Rice University News and Media.* 7 April 2012. http://news.rice.edu/2012/02/15/nanoparticles-may-enhance-cancer-therapy/.

[35] Taylor, Jill Bolte. *My Stroke of Insight: A Brain Scientist's Personal Journey.* New York: Viking, 2006.

[36] For a fascinating ontological/theological/philosophical discussion on this topic, visit http://livinginthequestion.posterous.com/the-question-of-oneness.

[37] Kurzweil, Ray. *The Singularity Is Near: When Humans Transcend Biology.* New York: Viking Penguin, 2005. p. 389.

[38] Dooling, Richard. *Rapture for the Geeks: When AI Outsmarts IQ.* New York: Harmony Books, 2008.

[39] Read his clever rewrite of Genesis at *http://www.richarddooling.com/index.php/2006/03/01/genesys-eula-for-the-universe/.*

ABOUT THE AUTHOR

Ogun R. Holder was ordained a Unity minister in 2011. His many titles include speaker, teacher, author, radio show host, blogger, musician, husband, parent, social media consultant and self-proclaimed geek. He is the executive director of Unity For All, a nonprofit on a mission of global transformation through spiritual education, empowerment and engagement (*www.unityforall.org*). His articles have been published in *Daily Word*®, *Unity Magazine*®, *Contact* magazine, and other Unity special publications.

Originally from Barbados, Holder moved to the United States in 1994 to pursue a degree in music therapy. As a music therapist, he worked successfully with a variety of populations in schools, hospitals, adult daycare facilities and his own private practice. He is also an experienced church music director, having served several Unity communities.

The author currently lives in the Washington, D.C., metro area with his wife, daughter and two dogs. To connect with him, visit *www.ogunholder.com* or *www.rantstorevs.com*.

Printed in the U.S.A. B0191